A Gentleman in khaki ordered South:
A Diary of the Transvaal War

Stephen Huggins

Stephen Huggins

ISBN: 10:1548705659
ISBN-13:978-1548705657

DEDICATION

To George Stokes and all the gentlemen in khaki who were ordered South, and to those they fought against, with hope for the healing of the nations.

When you've shouted "Rule Britannia": when you've sung "God Save the Queen
When you've finished killing Kruger with your mouth:
Will you kindly drop a shilling in my little tambourine
For a gentleman in khaki ordered South?
He's an absent-minded beggar and his weaknesses are great:
But we and Paul must take him as we find him:
He is out on active service wiping something off a slate:
And he's left a lot of little things behind him!
Duke's son – cook's son – son of a hundred kings,
(Fifty thousand horse and foot going to Table Bay!)
Each of 'em doing his country's work (and who's to look after the things?)
Pass the hat for your credit's sake, and pay – pay – pay!

From The Absent Minded Beggar, by Rudyard Kipling

Stephen Huggins

CONTENTS

Stephen Huggins

FORWARD

George Stokes' diary of his experiences during the Boer War came into my possession in Autumn 2016. In all probability it had begun its long journey to me simply through a house clearance. I understand that this is often the way in these matters. The diary was simply part of the effects that are left at the end of a person's life and, as such, have to be dealt with accordingly.

However, the diary is of great importance both sentimentally, of course, to George Stokes' family and also for a wider readership in terms of what may be learned from it. In this latter sense there are two key areas. First, it is often the case that the historical account of an event comes down from a fairly narrowly defined group whose position in society affords them power and control in these matters. So it is that in historical accounts of war the focus has been put on the account of those who were military leaders or politicians to the exclusion of most others. By contrast, until fairly recently, the experiences of those ordinary people who actually played the major part in those events has been largely ignored. George Stokes' diary goes towards redressing this imbalance as it provides the reader with a personal account of what it was like to be an ordinary soldier fighting in the Boer War. It is one man's account not only of the war's events but also of his personal thoughts, feelings and reflections on them.

The diary is also important because it is an artefact which sheds much light on Britain's imperial history. At the time of George Stokes' writing the British Empire cast a giant shadow on the world stage. For a Victorian soldier like George Stokes it may well have been difficult to conceive of a world in which the British Empire did not play a leading part, just as for those who live in post-imperialist Britain, it as it is as hard to conceive of one with it. There is much that the diary can teach us about our nation's past.

Stephen Huggins

ACKNOWLEDGMENTS

During the course of my work on the diary I was fortunate to make contact with Anthony Bagshaw, who is George Stokes' Great Grandson. Through Anthony, the family kindly gave permission for me to take the diary forward for publication. They also provided the photographs in this book and were a valuable source of much detailed material about George Stokes. I am very grateful to them for their generous sharing of their own family history with me, a stranger to them. The family had gathered a good deal of information about George Stokes but, interestingly, they knew nothing of the existence of his diary. It was a pleasure to inform them of the diary and what I was hoping to do with it. Following a telephone conversation with Anthony I came to realise that the diary should be returned to the family and this it was my joy to do. The diary that George Stokes carried with him all through his fighting in far off South Africa had finally come home.

I should also like to thank Lolly for all her invaluable help with this book.

The South African War, a man and his diary

The 2nd Anglo-Boer War 1899-1902

The war between Britain and the Boers of the Orange Free State and the Transvaal which took George Stokes to South Africa was the culmination of many years of conflict in the region.

The Dutch ancestors of the Boers had been in South Africa since 1652. They had settled and farmed there. The British arrived on the scene much later in 1795 when they established a presence in Cape Colony which they had taken over from the Dutch as part of the war against France. Not only did Cape Colony provide Britain with a toehold in the vast African continent but it was also of strategic importance as a place en route for India and the outposts of Empire in the Far East.

The Boers were a fiercely independent people whose lives had been fashioned both by the general harshness of their living conditions and also the ongoing conflict with local African tribes, especially the Zulus. The Boers were also much influenced in outlook by their profoundly Calvinistic expression of Christianity. Based on a particular understanding of the Bible, especially the Old Testament, they saw themselves as 'God's Chosen People'. As such they firmly held to the view that they had a divine right to treat and use black Africans, whom they believed to be inferior, as was felt fit.

This last issue of the treatment of their black African neighbours was to bring the Boers into conflict with the British. Ever since 1833 there had been a move within the Empire towards the emancipation of all enslaved peoples. This went against firmly held Boer views on such matters.

So it was that the Boers began to look for a greater degree of autonomy from British imperialist rule. Between 1835-37 as many as 5,000 Boers left the coastal region and ventured into the vast African interior in what has become known as the Great Trek.

The Boers' hopes to remove themselves from imperialist British influence were to be short lived with the discovery of diamonds near Kimberley in 1867. The desire to secure control and possession of such a valuable commodity sucked into the area thousands of incomers, many of whom were British, and soon these *Uitlanders*[1] outnumbered the local Boers. Tension between the Boers and British was understandably high and all attempts to reach a political solution failed.

The First Anglo-Boer War broke out in December 1880 over the imposition by the British of a hotly disputed tax on the Boers. The war lasted only some ten weeks but this was sufficient time for further embitterment on both sides. The Boers felt a sense of increased resentment at attempts by the British to have any degree of control over or involvement in their affairs. For their part the British were smarting at their loss of face in this short war.

In 1886 a second major mineral discovery, this time of gold, was made at Witwatersrand just some thirty miles from the Boer capital at Pretoria. British interests in the region became renewed as increasing numbers of *Uitlanders* arrived in search of their fortunes.

The political situation deteriorated even further in December 1895 with the so-called Jameson Raid. This was a miscalculated and ill-fated attempt by a British colonial, Leander Jameson, to lead a raid on

Johannesburg with the intention of inciting a general uprising of the *Uitlanders* who would then seize control. The raid was a singular failure and no uprising came about. However, the impact of the Jameson Raid on the political situation and contribution to the coming of war may not be understated. It certainly was the catalyst for further war. The point was well made by Jan Smuts some years after the war in 1906 'The Jameson Raid was the real declaration of war in the Great Anglo-Boer conflict...'[2]. When the British later defied a Boer ultimatum to cease their build up of forces in the region war became inevitable and on October 11th 1899 it began.

It would be true to say that the British were not well prepared for the coming of war in South Africa. There appears to have been a singular lack of necessary organisation and planning on their part.

British troops began to arrive in South Africa in 1899 where they were joined by soldiers from other parts of the Empire. The first phase of the war saw the Boers take the initiative as they invaded the British colonies of Natal and the Cape. The Boers besieged the key towns of Ladysmith, Mafeking and Kimberley. In the early stages of the war the British met with some degree of success at Talana and again at Elandslaagte but later suffered very significant defeats at Stormberg, Magersfontein and

Colenso closely together between 10th – 15th December 1899 in what became known as 'Black Week'. The news of the defeats and their associated loss of life had a shattering impact in Britain[3].

The situation was soon to be turned around by the British. Heavy troop reinforcements arrived and Lord Roberts[4] took overall command of the British forces with Lord Kitchener[5] becoming his Chief of Staff. By the end of February 1900 the sieges at both Kimberley and Ladysmith had been lifted and by the middle of May so, too, that at Mafeking. The British made further rapid military progress with the Orange Free State being annexed at the end of May. The following month the British also took Pretoria and so the Transvaal was annexed in September as well. It seemed that the war was nearly over. However, this was not to prove the case as it still had a long way to run[6].

The Boers moved to abandon the British style of military engagement and took to the use of guerrilla tactics, instead. This suited the Boers hugely as in so doing they were able to draw on their intimate knowledge and wide experience of the terrain on which they chose to operate. The Boers organised themselves into small and very mobile military units through which they sought not only to attack the British at their weakest points but also to disrupt their lines of communication and supply.

The British responded by adopting a scorched earth policy in which some 30,000 Boer farms were burnt with the aim of denying the Boers access to food. By March 1901 the British had also built about 8,000 blockhouses together with 3,700 miles of wire fencing all guarded by 50,000 troops with the intention of restricting Boer movement. What this tactic actually brought about was the displacement of huge numbers of Boer and black African families whom the British rounded up and placed in concentration camps[7]. The suffering and death toll in these camps was huge and brought much opprobrium around the world as well as at home in Britain. However, the use of the camps is largely seen as the key which brought the Boers to seek an end to the war in favour of the British. It ended officially on May 31st 1902 with the Peace of Vereeniging.

It is perhaps the case that because the 2nd Anglo-Boer War was concluded only a matter of twelve years before the First World War began it has subsequently become somewhat eclipsed both in terms of the national consciousness and also historical focus. In many ways this was to be rather inevitable. What could compare with the industrial scale death tolls, carnage and suffering of 1914-18?

Yet in its time the Boer War was of huge importance to Britain. It raised many profound questions on a range of issues which would reverberate down through the years. Because of the generally poor levels of fitness exhibited by the men called to serve in the Boer War the physical, and therefore it was assumed moral, state of the nation was strongly questioned. Around 40% of the men who volunteered to serve in the war were rejected on the grounds of being unfit for service while some 700 soldiers were shipped home as not being fit to fight. The grinding poverty which characterised the life of the poor had taken its toll[8].

At the same time, as the war progressed many of the previously widely held and long standing assumptions made about the organisation of the British Army were challenged, particularly over its capacity to adapt to new and different circumstances of warfare. It became clear that, despite a degree of reform[9] the late Victorian Army had not essentially changed its tactical attitudes in the face of hugely significant technological developments to weaponry and munitions.

The Boer War began in a widespread fervour of patriotism and bullish imperialism to be found expressed up and down the country and at all levels of society. However, the whole issue of the moral pursuit of Empire was laid bare when it became clear that in order to subdue the Boers finally their woman and children had been rounded up and placed in concentration camps with an appalling degree of death and suffering.

Not only did the Boer War raise such significant issues but victory in it came at a great cost to Britain. In the almost one hundred years from the end of the Napoleonic Wars until the start of the First World War there was no war to compare with the Boer War in terms of its length – two and three quarter years, spanning the reign of two British monarchs, Victoria and Edward VII. It was hugely expensive with a cost to the national exchequer of £200 million. The scale of the death toll in the war was vast with unprecedented figures for a single war involving the British Army[10].

The Boer War was hugely important for Britain on the international stage. Both America and Germany were now in a position to challenge Britain's world domination. In 1899 Britain was at the height of imperial power and so its inability to deal with a group of Boer farmers determined to resist that power made for uncomfortable times. Could the British Empire be maintained or would other rival powers seek to take advantage of the situation?

It is all no small wonder that no other than Kipling should add his voice to the national debate about where the Boer War had left the British people.

'Let us admit it fairly, as a business people should,
We have had no end of a lesson: it will do us no end
of good.'[11]

The Second Boer War was, of course, also greatly
significant to the peoples of South Africa on whose
land it had been fought. The loss of life and
suffering which it brought about were never to be
forgotten, while its outcome laid the political
blueprint for the future of the country and its
people, both black and white. It may well be true to
say that the Second Boer War singularly shaped the
history of South Africa in the twentieth century.

George Stokes

George Stokes was born in 1879 in Bulwell,
Nottinghamshire to William and Hannah Stokes. He
was the third of four brothers[12]. George's father was
a labourer and collier and so it is highly likely that
the family, like so many at the time, had little by the
way of money to support them. This may have been
the reason that led George to enlist on 3rd July
1895[13]. Though the pay of an ordinary soldier had
never been a great deal at least there were regular
meals and accommodation provided. It may have
seemed the better option. George's Army records,
in fact, show that he went to Northampton where he
was not known when he went to enlist and where he
assumed the alias of George Bramley in order to lie

about his age which he gave as just over 18 years. He was not. Whether it was money or another issue which prompted him George was keen to join up. In so doing it may be that this says much about his fortitude of character. At the age of just 16 George felt that he could hold his own in the very masculine world of the Victorian British Army. According to his enlistment record George was of fresh complexion with brown hair and blue eyes. He weighed 120 lbs and stood just a fraction over 5 foot 6 inches tall.

George's army career kept him in England before he left for South Africa on 21st October 1899. His service there went beyond the end of hostilities and the signing of peace terms as he did not return to this country until 2nd June 1903. He was finally discharged on 2nd July 1911.

George had an aptitude for the Army His records show that he gained Certificates of Education at 3rd Class and 2nd Class[14]. George also passed classes of instruction for those seeking to enter the ranks of Corporal and Sergeant[15]. He attained the rank of Corporal in November 1897 which again indicates much about the calibre of one so young in his years.

George's service records show that on 25th July 1900[16] he was tried by a Regimental Court Martial where he was sentenced to be reduced to the ranks.

There is no clear indication in the records to indicate what may have brought George to this situation. Perhaps it was at this point that his real identity and age had come to light? That George was on active service when all this happened may account for the reason that his Commanding Officer chose to remit the sentence.

George's service in the war earned him the Queen's South Africa medal together with clasps for Belmont, Modder River, the Orange Free State and the Transvaal. He was also awarded the King's South Africa medal with clasps for 1901 and 1902.

Not very long after George returned to Britain from South Africa he got married to Beatrice Eldred on 16th July 1903 in the parish church of St Peter & St Paul, Weedon Bec, near Daventry, Northamptonshire. George was 24 and a labourer, while Beatrice was 28.

In the following years George and Beatrice had 6 children. George took up employment as a Deputy at Carlow Colliery and also at the Staveley Coal and Iron Company[17].

At the outbreak of World War 1 George rejoined the Army. His enlistment papers show that he joined the 11th (Service) Battalion Sherwood Foresters at Derby on 9th September 1914 aged 35 years. The war was by then only a few weeks old[18].

As one of the first to rise to serve his country it again says much about his character. Presumably on account of his previous military service George was immediately promoted that same day to the rank of sergeant. He stayed in England until 27th August 1915 when he was sent to France to fight remaining there until 19th December 1915 when he came home. Back in England George was involved in training soldiers at camps on Cannock Chase, Staffordshire and at Clipston, Nottinghamshire. George finally attained the rank of Company Sergeant Major. It is salutary to see the effect that the war had on George when comparing his two photographs, one from 1914, the other from 1918. The war seems to have aged him much as it surely must have done so many men, at least, those fortunate enough to have survived.

In 1919 George left the Army being discharged as Class Z Reserve and returned to civilian life again working in mining. According to family anecdote come the outbreak of hostilities in 1939 George sought enlistment in the Army for a third time, though by now he was aged 60.Unsurprisingly, his application was denied but once again it demonstrates the character of the man.

George Stokes died on 10th January 1953 aged 74 years. He is buried with his wife, Beatrice, in Spital Cemetery, Chesterfield.

Diary of the Transvaal War

The Diary

George Stokes' diary of the Transvaal War must have been of much value to him.

On its front paper is still listed the price of 2s 6d[19] which he paid at a time when a soldier in the late Victorian Army earned the traditional 1/- a day[20].

The purchase of the diary represents quite some investment of a young man's limited financial resources.

That the diary was important to Stokes may further be seen in that he had it with him, among the limited range of personal items permitted, together with all his kit when he embarked from England bound for South Africa in October1899. Stokes then carried the diary with him throughout the campaign making almost daily entries. When he returned home in 1903 he brought it with him and kept it.

The diary has board covers which are secured by a brass clap. It measures 7 by 4 ½ half inches and weighs 9 ½ ounces. All 187 of its pages are filled with Stokes' record of his war.

As with many diarists of the nineteenth century Stokes wrote in pencil[21]. Pen and ink would have been impracticable on active service on the veldt. His handwriting is beautifully shaped in a flowing style common to those schooled in the Victorian school system. It is astonishingly neatly accomplished given the circumstances in which it was written. Stokes also had very good use of spelling, punctuation and grammar[22] and, as such, the diary is easy to read. The introduction of universal education in 1870 had done much to raise literacy levels in the nation and Stokes had clearly shared in this. The British soldiers who fought in this war were far more literate than any of their predecessors. As Stokes held the rank of Corporal he was further required to demonstrate a higher degree of literacy. The general rise in literacy also did much to popularise diary keeping across many areas of society[23].

Stokes' diary keeping pays careful attention to detail. There is much reference to dates, times of day and to distances[24]. Local names of places are accurately recorded as is the use of unfamiliar Afrikaans words[25]. There is also verbatim recording of published Army Orders and speeches by officers[26]. All such factors remarkable given Stokes' background.

The diary, quite naturally, reflects what was important to its author. It provides a valuable insight into the lot of the Victorian soldier on active service. Like many of his fellows throughout the years Stokes complains at the treatment and attitude of the officers towards the men[27] and of the harshness of their conditions[28]. At the same time it is touching to read of Stokes' pleasure at receiving the Queen Victoria gift chocolate box at Christmas 1899[29] and similarly of meeting his cousin who was also serving with the Army in South Africa[30].

Stokes' diary reflects, of course, late Victorian attitudes to issues such as race[31] but it could do no other. However, what is most significantly lacking in the diary is any degree of antipathy towards the Boers. They are often referred to simply as 'the enemy'. At the same time the diary reveals most clearly and, indeed, graphically, the attitude of a professional soldier who knew what was necessary to get his job done[32].

Footnotes - The Second Anglo-Boer War, 1899-02

1. 'Uitlander' is an Afrikaans word which means 'foreigner' or 'outlander'. Exact figures are not known as to how many Uitlanders had come into the region. It is estimated that their number was at least equal to that of the Boers and some take the view that they were in a majority.

2. Jan Smuts was widely involved in the fighting of the Second Boer War and showed particular tactical awareness in the guerrilla stage of the war. Smuts was legal adviser to the Transvaal in the peace talks. He became Prime Minister of the Union of South Africa and late also a Field Marshall in the British Army.

3. The British public was used to its army being successful in the field and expected no less in this conflict. The Boers were a small citizen army while the British forces were both professional and well equipped. The loss of 2, 776 men killed wounded or captured in such a short space of time filled the nation with gloom and embarrassment. However, at the same time, from a military perspective these reverses also had a

positive impact in that many thousands of men now clamoured to volunteer for service in South Africa.

4. Like many, Stokes held Lord Roberts in high regard. For example, see his diary entry for 19th May 1900.

5. Horatio Kitchener served in the Nile Expedition (1884-5), Suakin (1888) and won acclaim for winning the Battle of Omdurman (1898) which restored The Sudan to Egypt. Lord Kitchener later became Secretary of War during World War 1.

6. Stokes' diary entry for 7th June 1900 shows that he shared this optimistic view.

7. Although it is widely said that the British use of concentration camps in the Boer War was the first in history this is not the case as they had been used by both the Americans and the Spanish in the Philippine-American War which ran concurrently from 1899-02. Where the British use of the camps was singular was in their scale and number. The vast majority of the Boer prisoners herded into the camps were women and children of whom some 26, 000 were to die. The British also removed black workers from Boer

18

farms on which they worked and interned them in camps as well with more than 20, 000 perishing. Whatever their purpose the use of the concentration camps is a shameful episode in British history.

8. Concern for this situation became a focus for the attention of late Victorian philanthropy. Writing in *The Bitter Cry of Outcast London* about his investigation into housing conditions in Bermondsey in 1883 the Reverend Andrew Mearns reported 'Few who read these pages have any conception of what these pestilential human rookeries are where thousands are crowded together amidst horrors which call to mind the what we have heard of the middle passage of the slave ship.'

9. As Secretary of State for War (1868-74) Edward Cardwell had shaken the British Army to its foundations with a series of radical reforms. Cardwell abolished the purchase of commissions by officers and also introduced short service for the men in the ranks. Cardwell was further responsible for the introduction of the linked battalion system and the localisation of regiments. He also abolished flogging, increased the pay and generally improved the conditions of the

common soldier. The reform of the Army continued with Hugh Childers, a later Secretary of War who brought about a wide degree of change to the regimental system.

10. Some 22, 000 British soldiers were killed in the war of which only 35% died in battle with the majority perishing from disease. At least 7, 000 Boer troops were also killed while around 26, 000 Boer women and children died in the concentration camps. Significantly , at the time no detailed figures were kept by the British of the native Africans or 'Black Boers', as they were sometimes called, who died , though it may have been around 12, 000. An untold number of native Africans called to support the British war effort were killed by the Boers.

11. From his poem *The Lesson* (1901).

George Stokes

12. According to the 1881 Census, when George was two years old, the family was living in Radford, Nottinghamshire. By the time of the 1891 Census they were living in Cossall, also in Nottinghamshire.

13. It was clearly a day that meant something to George as he includes reference to its anniversary in his diary entry for 3rd July 1900.

14. He achieved the 3rd Class Certificate on 6th October 1896 and the 2nd Class Certificate on 26th April 1897.

15. George passed his class of instruction for the rank of Corporal on 29th June 1898 and for that of Sergeant on 15th December 1898.

16. This was not an uncommon feature of the ordinary soldier's life.

17. The company was based in Chesterfield and was involved in the quarrying of ironstone, coal mining and chemical production.

18. Britain had declared war on Germany on 4th August 1914. George Stokes re-enlisted a little more than four weeks later.

The Diary

19. The cost of the diary is approximately £14.00 by values of today.

20. Although reforms to the conditions of

ordinary soldiers in this period had improved their pay was still low. A day's pay would be around £6.50 by today's values.

21. For a soldier on active service the use of a pencil makes good practical sense. As a medium for writing the pencil has been much favoured by diarists over the years. For example, Nella Last who contributed her diary entries to the Mass Observation for many years wrote everything in pencil.

22. Though it is interesting to note that, except for their correct use in abbreviations, there are no full stops but only commas in the diary.

23. Advances in working class literacy had contributed to a growth in the popularity of diary writing among those from Victorian society who may well have not had opportunity to do so before

24. For example, see Stokes' diary entry for 30th May 1900.

25. For example, see Stokes' diary entry for 18th May 1900.

26. For example, see Stokes' diary entry for 10th

February 1900 and 21st May 1900.

27. For example, see Stokes' diary entry for 21st May 1900.

28. For example, see Stokes' diary entry for 16th March 1900.

29. See Stokes' diary entry for 26th January 1900.

30. For example, see Stokes' diary entry for 27th December 1899 and 10th February 1900.

31. See Stokes' diary entry for 14th November 1899.

32. See Stokes' diary entry for 25th November 1899.

Diary of the Transvaal War[1]

Dear Friends in commencing this diary I must begin from the time of landing in South Africa & to give you a clear understanding I must tell you I belong to the "2nd. Battalion Northamptonshire Reg."[2]

14th November 1899

We arrived in Cape Town[3] on the morning of the 14th November 1899 at 4pm and we disembarked at 5pm. We had tea on the landing stage. Tea comprised of biscuits and tinned beef and tea. At 5 30pm each officer, NC Officer and private was issued with an emergency ration which we were strictly ordered not to touch unless ordered to do so by an officer. We were then served out with 3 days ration each which composed of biscuit and tinned beef. About 6pm we fell in dressed in our accoutrements and carrying a great coat on our back and a blanket rolled and carried like a sack over the right shoulder. After the roll had been called and inspection over we were then marched through the customs shed to the train which was waiting to convey us up country. We were then told off in eights and each eight sent to the compartment allocated to them. A saloon carriage was reserved for our officers. When all was ready the whistle blew but before the train could move an orderly came up with two bags of letters etc. for us which had arrived in by the mail boat that day from England. The bags were put on the train and we started our long ride up country. Received a hearty send-off from the people of Cape Town. It was laughable to see the natives dancing and shouting amongst the Europeans. After leaving Cape Town there was nothing to be seen but the wide expanse of veldt dotted with a native's kraal here and there. Darkness came on soon after we left Cape Town so we unrolled our blankets and settled down to sleep as best we could.

15th November 1899

I woke up quite refreshed after a good night's rest to find the sun shining gloriously and the train whirling us along past mountains and farmhouses. I had my food during the day when I felt I should like a bite for I had nothing which required cooking. We stopped at several stations which were of no comment but we refilled our water bottles at some of them. At about 5pm we stopped at a station named Wellington[4]. It was a pretty little station and the platform was crowded with people waiting our arrival and waving Union Jacks. As soon as possible we detrained and some water was quickly boiled and we had tea. After tea we entrained again and in my compartment we found a small packet and on opening it we found 1 packet of tea, 1 packet of cigarettes, 1 pen and a pencil and three boxes of matches and a small card was inscribed 'With best wishes from the inhabitants of Wellington'. On making enquiries I found a similar packet had been put in every compartment. It was very good of those people and declared their loyalty to the Queen and we were all very grateful to them. On leaving Wellington we were heartily cheered. Darkness soon came over and we settled down again for another night's sleep in the train.

16th November 1899

I awakened about 6am and the sun was shining lovely and after having a little to eat settled down to read and now and again putting reading aside to gaze through the window at the fine scenery for all around for miles were large kopjes such as I had never seen before so I was naturally interested in them. About 2pm we stopped at De Aar[5] and detrained for dinner. There is nothing to say about De Aar for it was only a small station and a few troops were guarding and they were the first troops we had seen since leaving Cape Town. I was told we had only got about another 20 miles to go to reach our destination. About 2 30pm we left De Aar and half an hour later we crossed the Orange River[6] and saw a number of white tents which told us that troops were encamped there. We stopped alongside a large kopje and detrained and after we had taken all baggage, stores etc. from the train we marched to the camp. Having took off our accoutrements we pitched our tents alongside the "King's Own Yorkshire Light Infantry Reg." and settled down to rest. I will now explain what we were forming there, and the various regiments concerned. The regiments concerned were :- "2nd Northamptonshire Reg.", "King's Own Yorkshire Light Infantry Reg.", "5th Northumberland Infusiliers" and half the "North Lancashire Reg." the whole forming the 9th Brigade commanded by General Pole-Carew[7]. One "Battalion Scots Guards", 2nd Battalion "Coldstream Guards" and 1st Battalion "Grenadier Guards" comprised the Guards Brigade commanded by General Featherstonehaugh. 2 batteries of R.A., 9th Lancers, 1 company of A.S.C., 1 company of R.E., a detachment of "sailors" and "marines" with naval guns completed the1st Division commanded by General Lord Methuen[8]. The object of the division was to march up country to the 'Relief of Kimberley' so were termed 'The Kimberley Relief Force'.

17th November 1899

The arrival of the naval detachment today from H.M.S. Doris[9] completed the division and we were ready to march.

21st November 1899

Nothing worth mentioning has occurred since the 17th inst. Only the ordinary camp life, doing Outpost Duty, Fatigues etc. At 3am this morning the division struck camp and half an hour later we started our march up country to the Relief of Kimberley being about 12,000 strong. We carried nothing with us except our accoutrements with 100 rounds of ammunition in the pouches per man and rifles, our coats and blankets were carried on waggons drawn by mules. We arrived at a place called Wittiputts Farm[10] about 11am and halted for the day. We soon had dinner and got down to bed.

22nd November 1899

We left Wittiputts Farm at 2pm and halted for the night at about 8pm within 4 miles of Belmont[11] and bivouacked alongside a small kopje. After we had taken our accoutrements off we went and filled our water bottles at a pond amidst a tumult of mules kicking and splashing in the dark at the same pond. Afterwards we had tea and bread and jam. We then got our blankets off the wagons and I soon rolled myself up in mine and went to sleep.

23rd November 1899

We were wakened up and told to get ready for moving off but to make as little noise as possible. It was then pitch dark and must have been about 2am. At about 3am we started and strictly ordered not to talk or smoke. About an hour later we were intended for an attack and my heart began to quicken its beating at the thoughts of a fight and it being my baptism of fire, as it was the majority of us, we opened out in a long line and about 8 paces distance between each man so as to present as small a target as possible to the enemy. We were the first line and the 5th Infusiliers the second line, the K.O.Y.L.I. and the N. Lancs. Regiment being in reserve. The Guards Brigade being in a similar position were on our right and in that order we steadily advanced across the open plain towards a large kopje we could see as it was just breaking day. As we crossed the railway line we became aware of the ping, zip, whew of the bullets as some whistled past us and others struck the ground at our feet and now and again we could hear the deep boom of the big guns. A slight pause on our part caused by the sudden hail of bullets and then on we pushed, stooping down and marching forward with the noise of the bullets sounding in our ears but luckily for us it wasn't very light and their shooting was bad on that account but as neared the foot of the kopje one of our Captains was hit in the right ankle and was the first to fall. We scrambled up the sides of the kopje closely followed by the 5th Fusiliers who had suffered heavily behind us. Half way up the kopje we were ordered to fix bayonets and amidst the sounds of the beating of a side drum and the notes from a bugle we anxiously awaited the order to charge, but we were not allowed to do so as the enemy fled to take up another position further back so we unfixed bayonets and retired down the kopje and went round the foot of it. Meantime the Guards Brigade having gone round the right engaged the enemy when they retired to the 2nd kopje and drove them off in a short space of time and they retired to a 3rd kopje. Now to return to the 9th Brigade. After going round the foot of the 1st kopje they advanced after the Guards Brigade leaving my company and a few men of other regiments who had missed with us, engaged with a party of the enemy who had been cut off from their force on its retiring and were behind huge rocks sniping at us and we could not see them but we fired at random where we saw the smoke issuing from their rifles and after about half an hour of sharp firing they hoisted the white flag and some of our men stood up but were immediately shot down. We then commenced blazing at them again and the white flag fell but was immediately hoisted again and we were ordered to cease firing but to remain flat on the ground and in a few minutes we had the pleasure of seeing the cowardly hounds file out from behind the rocks and lay down their arms and we took them prisoners, 20 in all. During the time we were so engaged the Division had attacked and successfully taken the 3rd kopje at the point of the bayonet causing the enemy to retire as fast as they could over the veld leaving some of their dead and wounded on the kopje. Thus ended our first battle which was a glorious victory after 8 hours severe fighting. The regiments were then all formed up to march back to the camp we left, traversing the battle field on our way we saw the plain dotted here and there with the bodies of the brave fellows who had lost their lives and the mule wagons picking them up to convey them to camp for burial. Soon after reaching camp we had dinner and afterwards buried the dead. Then we lay down for a hard earned rest. The casualties of my regiment were 2 captains, 1 Lieutenant, 19 N.C.O and Privates wounded. 50 of the enemy were taken prisoners in all and one of them was shot for treacherously using the white flag. The station-master at Belmont also was shot as a traitor for giving information to the enemy regarding our movements. We could not ascertain the loss on the enemy's side as they carried most of their dead and wounded with them as they are all mounted on horses.

24th November 1899

We started on the march just before daybreak and marched about 12 miles and then bivouacked for the remainder of the day and night.

25th November 1899

About 2 30am we moved forward again and in a short time the scouts who were ahead of us returned with the news that the enemy were in a strong position on a large kopje and in great strength at a place called Graspan[12] about 3 miles ahead of us so we proceeded with caution some distance and then formed for attack. The 9th Brigade formed the attacking force and the Guards Brigade formed the reserves. The K.O.Y.L.I. and the Naval Brigade formed the 1st line, the 2nd Northampton Regiment and the half battalion N. Lancs Regiment the 2nd line, the 5th Fusiliers came in reserve. In this formation we pushed forward and very soon we heard the boom of the big guns and knew that our guns were shelling the enemy's position. Soon after we came in range of the enemy's fire and the bullets began to spit and splatter around us and in a very short space of time the ground around us was covered with dead and wounded from the 1st line. After about 2 hours as near as I could guess the 2nd line rushed forward to reinforce the 1st line as they had lost so heavily. About this time 3 big guns were brought into action on the plain in rear of us and commenced firing over our heads at the point of the kopje we were attacking. After the guns had kept up a constant fire for a considerable time we were ordered to fix bayonets and climb the kopje as soon as the big guns had ceased firing. After waiting anxiously for some time we began the climb, scrambling over huge rocks and dead and wounded as they fell. It was a terrible climb and one I shall never forget for as I neared the top a bullet passed through the left sleeve of my jacket but there was no time to think of that for with a last effort we all reached to the top and the enemy fled but a great many who could not get away had 9 inches of cold steel. Some of them threw their rifles down and asked for mercy. They got it very soon. When we had finished with those we caught on the kopje we lay down utterly exhausted after 9 hours severe fighting and we could hear our R.A. guns sending shells after the enemy as parting shots and to help them along as the 9th Lancers' horses were too exhausted to pursue them. Thus ended our second battle and victory but at a great cost for as we retired down the kopje we saw the plain literally covered with dead and also the side of the kopje, the wounded having been taken away to the ambulances by the stretcher bearers. I saw no less than 20 dead bodies within a radius of 35 yards, the majority of them being men of the Naval Brigade and some of them were ghastly sights and past recognition. I spoke to a sailor who said he was looking for his chum who he thought had fell. He himself had got 6 bullet holes through his clothing but had not been scratched. It was about this time that Guards Brigade appeared on the scene for they had not been required in the fighting. We bivouacked about a mile from the scene of the fight and a great number of the troops rode that mile on horses which we captured a large number from the Boers. After dinner we lay down to rest and at 5pm we buried the killed. The dead bodies are sewn up in blankets and carried shoulder high to their last resting place and laid in large graves of 20 and over more in each grave. It is an impressive sight and one never to be forgotten. The water we had to drink here was very dirty and we had to clinch our teeth when drinking to prevent us swallowing the dirt and various insects which were in it. Our food up to now had been chiefly hard biscuits and tinned meat which is better known to Tommy A.[13] as "Bully Beef" because of its inferior quality. The casualties of my regiment were 1 Private killed and 23 N.C.O. and Privates wounded. The other regiments in the fighting suffered more severe. The K.O.Y.L.I. and Naval Brigade having the most casualties. Lord Methuen said the enemy had suffered great loss.

26th November 1899

Lord Methuen allowed us to rest all day and pull ourselves together as we needed a little recreation after the two hard fights.

27th November 1899

We started on the march again just before daybreak and halted at a farm within 3 miles of Modder River[14]. Outposts were thrown out and we settled down to rest.

28th November 1899

We advanced to our 3rd battle which proved to be the longest and fiercest of the three lasting as it did 15 hours. The enemy were strongly entrenched along the river bank (south side) and having been reinforced were in large numbers. About daybreak the R.A. began to shell the enemy and we advanced under their cover in extended order and when within rifle range we were ordered to lie down and commence firing. In this position we lay for several hours with the bullets falling like hailstones around us but we kept a steady fire directed upon the enemy and the men of the R.A.S. Corps and stretcher bearers were constantly employed in carrying the wounded to the rear from the firing line. The dead were of course allowed to remain where they lay as all possible help was required for the wounded. One after another of the stretcher bearers fell and others took their places. About mid-day a shout went up and it passed along the line that the enemy had retired across the river but only to occupy some more trenches on the north bank of the river. We were then ordered to advance in rushes and occupy the trenches the enemy had vacated which we did in the face of a withering rifle fire. It was in so doing that a great many brave fellows lost their lives including the Colonel of the Coldstream Guards and a Major of the same Corps. Who were leading their men in the rush. As the Colonel fell he shouted "Push on boys. Never mind me" and with a cheer we gained the trenches and went on with the firing. It was about this time that we were reinforced by the A & S Highlanders who had come up country by train. The Grenadier Guards on the right, the A & S Highlanders in the centre and the K.O.Y.L.I. were ordered to cross the river at given points. The Guards on getting halfway across were driven back but the A & S Highlanders and the K.O.Y.L.I. were successful for after a hard and terrible struggle they reached the opposite bank with a ringing cheer and rushed for the trenches but the sight of the bayonets struck terror amongst the Boers for they turned and rushed pell-mell across the plain in utter disorder and completely demoralised and fairly beat by the boys in khaki who were like drowned rats through crossing the river. Thus ended that long and terrible battle which was afterwards spoken of as one of the longest and fiercest ever fought in the annals of war[15]. The enemy did terrible executions amongst us with a quick firing gun which we called the pom-pom[16]. Their sharp shooters were perched in the trees but were picked off one by one by our troops. The Boer trenches were strewn with their dead and wounded and the latter were taken prisoner but the former were buried by us before going into camp. A great number of the enemy's horses were killed during the fight. Our losses were very severe. The brunt of the fighting was borne by the Grenadier Guards, the K.O.Y.L.I. and the A & S 2b. The casualties of my Regiment were luckily only 9 N.C.O. and Men wounded. We went into camp on the South side of the river just as darkness was coming on.

29th November 1899

We were all up at 6am but not very much refreshed after the night's rest for taking in all we had marched 50 miles, fought 3 three battles, all victories, and suffered great privations from the intense heat (& scarcity of water for we didn't wash during the whole time) in 8 days. We only had 1lb of bread during that time and that was the first day. The rest of the time we had hard biscuit & "Bully Beef". At 9am all the Divisions paraded for Lord

Methuen's inspection. The General made a speech. He said that he was proud of the troops under his command and would willingly lead them anywhere for we had suffered greatly but always cheerful and we had more than earned the rest which he was going to give us and which would be a fortnight & you can rest assured we were all pleased to hear it. In the afternoon tents came up the line on trains and we had them pitched as soon as possible and prepared to settle down for our long rest.

30th November 1899

Orders were issued as to the daily routine of camp life. "Reveille" would sound at 5am, "Retreat" at 6pm, "Tattoo" at 8 30pm, "Lights out" at 8 45pm. Each regiment to furnish the outposts in turn. Outposts would go out at 6pm and remain out until 6 30am. 3 miles from camp towards the north, the enemy were known to have retired to Magersfontein[17] and had taken up position on a large kopje called Scholtz Nek[18] about 8 miles from our camp. We were to have a parade from 7am to 8am for physical drill to keep us exercised every morning except Sundays. We were allowed to bathe in the Modder River after the dead Boers had been got out which numbered about 180 nearly all weighted down with rocks. They had been thrown in to prevent their actual losses being known. During the afternoon the "Black Watch" and the

"Highland L. Infantry" arrived by train and joined the "A. & S. H." to form the Highland Brigade so as to replace our casualties.

1st December 1899

At 9am "G" Coy. To which I belong and "A" Coy. "2nd Northamptons" under Captain Godley, Lieut. Brierly and Lieut. Wyndowe proceeded by train to "Enslin" a small station close to the scene of the Grass Pan fight to guard the railway and keep communication open with Belmont. Our total strength was 3 Officers, 200 N.C.O.'s & Men. On reaching "Enslin" we immediately proceeded to barricade the Station House by pulling out the windows and substituting iron railway sleepers leaving loop-holes to fire through.

2nd December 1899

About mid-day the "Seaforth Highlanders" passed through by train to Modder River and their arrival there completed the Highland Brigade under the command of General Wauchope[19]. We were at work the greater part of the day making breastworks and digging trenches around the house.

5th December 1899

Nothing to write about.

About the 3rd & 4th December 1899

Only the usual digging trenches etc. and ½ Coy. each day on Outpost Duty on a small kopje about 300 yards to the right of the railway. The house was situated on the left of the railway. To-night at about 11pm we were roused up by hearing shots fired from the kopje and we immediately lined the trenches ready for any visitors that might come. A Sergeant and 6 Ptes. Were sent over to the kopje to ascertain the cause of the shots and came back with the news that the sentry had heard strange sounds on the sides of the kopje and receiving no answer to his repeated challenge he fired 7 shots in succession from his magazine but nothing further was heard so we lay down again but with strict orders to keep on the alert. We was not disturbed again during the night.

6th December 1899

On the relieving outpost going up the kopje they found a dead bullock with 5 holes in its body so we came to the conclusion that was the poor unfortunate thing that disturbed the sentry. Hard lines for the bullock as it wasn't able to answer the sentry's challenge so it suffered accordingly. The sentry was a good shot at any rate and one of the enemy would have stood a poor chance I think.

7th December 1899

The 2 sections which means a ½ Coy. who were on outpost duty were ½ of "C" and their tour of duty ended at 6am but at 4 30am just at daybreak they were suddenly awakened to the fact that they were being attacked by the report of a gun and a shell flying overhead and which struck the further side of the kopje and scattering pieces of rock in all directions. The alarm was at once given and they were reinforced by a section of "A" Coy. who brought a box of ammunition with them. Meanwhile we had seized our rifles and lay down flat behind the rocks and commenced to play them at their own game, firing from behind rocks. When it was quite daylight we could plainly see our enemy who were from 1,000 to 1,100 strong and possessed a field gun which they repeatedly used, firing shrapnel shot from it but which luckily didn't do much damage. One shell struck the blankets and coat which were rolled up and was the property of Lance-Corporal B. Sharpe who is a Drummer and shattered them to pieces scarcely a moment after the owner had placed them there. The owner has still the coat in his possession. About 6 30am 3 men and a Lce-Corpl. brought us 3 camp kettles full of hot coffee from the house regardless of the bullets which struck the ground all around them but none of them were hit so half of us had a drink of coffee while the

41

other half kept up a hot fire on the enemy and then vice-versa. About 8am the cooks began to make coffee for breakfast but had to abandon the task and run for the trenches as a shell came and dropped amongst them but luckily without bursting. Shortly afterwards the enemy blew the line up and cut the telegraph wires on the south side of the house and so cut off all communications with Belmont. The captain who had wired to Modder River for reinforcements had just received an answer when the wires were cut towards the north cutting off communication in that direction, but they were too late for our situation had been made known and the enemy found out their mistake when it was too late, that must have made them for they favoured us with a perfect hail of bullets and 6 of our men were struck and a shell went over our heads and struck the door-way of the house smashing the woodwork to splinters but luckily no one was near it. This went on for several hours and our ammunition was rapidly running short and we began to fear the worst as there was no signs of reinforcements but we stuck to our guns and waited for the end to come which we thought must be soon when suddenly we espied a large body of men coming over a ridge on the plain towards us and we immediately cheered and shouted ourselves hoarse for we knew they were reinforcements and our end had not come. As they drew near we recognised the 9th Lancers and a

Battery of R.A. coming on at a gallop and waving their helmets so we placed ours on the rifles and waved in response. The enemy who must have seen the reinforcements as soon as us turned tail and fled across the plain but the R.A. came into action and sent a few shells after them and the 9th Lancers pursued them for a few miles and then returned. Shortly afterwards 4 Coy's of the Seaforth Highlanders marched up under General Wauchope who complimented us on the plucky stand we had made. We had kept the enemy at bay 8 ½ hours when reinforcements arrived. Our total casualties were :- 11 N.C.O.'s & Ptes. wounded and 2 Rimington Scouts[20] who were with us were also wounded. Out of the reinforcements 1 Artilleryman was wounded and also a Lieut. of the Lancers, making a total of 1 Officer, 14 N.C.O. & Ptes. wounded. Two of our wounded have since died. We could not ascertain the loss of the Boers but we found 2 of them severely wounded and one of them died immediately his wounds were dressed. We afterwards heard from some Boer prisoners that they had 19 killed and a number wounded. Their intention was to take our stores etc. but they took pills[21] instead.

8th December 1899

We were employed all day in repairing damages done to the trenches, breastworks etc. and generally strengthening the place. The Seaforth Highlanders stayed with us but the R.A. and 9th Lancers left at a late hour for Modder River.

9th December 1899

A Canadian contingent arrived here about mid-day to relieve us. They were about 800 strong and had a Maxim Gun with them so the enemy would have a warm reception if they attacked the place again. At 4 30pm we left Enslin and accompanied the Seaforth Highlanders to Modder River and there joined our regiment and received the congratulations of them all for our plucky stand.

10th December 1899

At about 3 30am the whole division including the Highland Brigade set out to attack the enemy at Magersfontein. The Highland Brigade having arrived since the Battle of Modder River and so being fresher than the other brigades were selected to make the attack. The remaining two brigades being held in reserve. The Highland Brigade advanced in quarter column and by some dreadful mistake went too far in that formation for they became entangled in barbed wire about 200 yards in advance of the Boers' trenches. In less time than it takes me to write it everywhere was utter confusion, shouting and yelling as the poor fellows tried to extend and extricate themselves from the barbed wire amidst a perfect hail of bullets from the Boer trenches. It was a terrible sight for the flashes from the enemy's rifles lit up the whole scene and we could see the poor fellows being literally mowed down with the bullets like grass before a scythe and the moans and cries of the wounded rent the air. It was awful but we could not help them. Suddenly above the din and rattle of musketry the one cry "Retire" rang out and those of the Highland Brigade that could do so came running towards us almost panic stricken. The 9th Brigade were immediately ordered to advance and cover the retreat of the Highland Brigade which we did and lay flat on the ground. As daylight approached we could plainly see the enemy in their trenches and all day long we lay thus scarcely daring to move. Now and again during the day a wounded Highlander could be seen crawling towards our lines and they were helped in at great risk. As darkness came on we were relieved by the Guards Brigade and we returned to camp.

11th December 1899

During the forenoon one of the enemy came forward to our lines with a flag of truce for ambulances, doctors etc. to fetch our dead and wounded to our own lines as the enemy could not attend to them being short of medical aid. It was a sorrowful task and many a tear was shed amongst us and during the afternoon we buried the dead amidst painful scenes. At 5pm the remnant of the Highland Brigade buried their brave general, General Wauchope who was riddled with bullet wounds being one of the first to fall. It was a terrible reverse caused by a great mistake which it is to be hoped will be explained when the war is over. It is not known who gave the order to "Retire" and may never be known. It is believed that had the order not been given the Highland Brigade would have taken the position with less loss of life. I cannot describe the awful scene as it really was so I will leave it to war correspondents who are more skilled in describing such scenes than I am. Our successful advance to the besieged Kimberley[22] was checked while the people there were anxiously awaiting our arrival which they were shortly expecting and hoping for.

12th December 1899

We again settled down to camp life for our advance to Kimberley was checked till we got reinforcements. The Naval Brigade with their gun which we christened "Joey Chamberlain"[23] and which was in position at a gangers hut on the railway line about 5 miles south of the Boers' position sent a few shells at their position at daybreak and then again in the evening about dusk.

17th December 1899

Nothing has occurred since the 12th inst. worth noting excepting the usual shelling daily by "Joey" at the enemy's position. This morning we went out of camp and made a reconnaissance of the enemy's position at daybreak. Our artillery got well within range and shelled them and they replied with their big guns dropping a few of their shells amongst our artillery without doing any damage as they didn't explode and the drivers simply ducked their heads and laughed at them. A few of their shells also dropped very close to Lord Methuen and his staff who retired a short distance out of range. After about 2 hours we returned to camp with the satisfaction of knowing we hadn't any casualties during the reconnaissance.

18th, 19th & 20th December 1899

The usual routine of camp life, outpost duty, fatigues etc. and the early morning "Coffee" for the enemy from our Naval Gun "Joey" daily.

21st December 1899

The usual work all day and turned in to sleep at 8 30pm. About 11pm the whole camp was awakened by the sound of a hearty rattle of musketry but as the alarm didn't sound we went to sleep again.

22nd December 1899

In making enquiries I heard that firing which disturbed us the previous night came from the enemy's trenches who were in constant dread of a night attack for on the least thing disturbing their sleep they seized their rifles and blazed away at the wide world and hit nothing but the ground. It didn't disturb our general much for he didn't trouble to strengthen the outposts. It's doubtful whether he got out of his bed or not.

23rd December 1899

We held divisional sports and all together we had a very good day. There was foot racing, long jumping, high jumping, hurdle jumping, tent pegging, driving competitions, sword combats, bayonet fighting and numerous other events and to wind up the day we had football and cricket contests. Lord Methuen gave a silver cup to the winning teams of the latter contests.

24th December 1899

We were treated to some good boxing bouts which took place on a raised platform put up for the purpose. Blood flowed freely during some of the bouts for Tommy knows how to fight with Nature's weapons as well as rifles and swords and is a fair glutton for punishment so there was a great deal of hard punching and finally black eyes and swelled noses were to be seen all over the camp. I was one of the spectators and enjoyed the whole day much.

25th December 1899

Xmas Day. Being Xmas Day all the troops were granted a general holiday. At 12 noon the whole Division turned out and gave three cheers for Her Majesty the Queen with uncovered heads[24]. I was unfortunately taken ill and had to go into hospital. I was admitted into the 9th Brigade Hospital in the afternoon. The troops had nothing extra for dinner but at night they received 1 quart of beer a man by paying 1/- but everyone was satisfied for the beer was a luxury in itself. Being in hospital I did not get any beer but I had two small sponge cakes for Tea. We had a severe sandstorm during the day which lasted about 3 hours and then went away leaving everything covered with sand.

26th December 1899

The doctor came and saw me about 9am. and said that I should be sent down the country to receive better treatment than they could give me. My food consisted of milk and beef tea.

27th December 1899

About 11am. I was taken and put in the Hospital Train with a lot more patients, some of them being wounded cases from Magersfontein battle. For dinner I had beef tea with a little bread soaked in it. We arrived at De Aar about 5pm. and was taken into hospital there and put to bed.

I must now pass over a number of dates as I was kept in hospital till the 21st January 1900 when I was discharged to the convalescent camp but I must tell you a little of what occurred during my stay in hospital. I had the pleasure of receiving a visit from my cousin who had arrived at De Aar that morning from Maitland with the ammunition column. Of course, I was very glad indeed to see him so soon after his arrival in this country for he only arrived on the 29th December/99. He was also very pleased to see me and he sat on my bed and told me about how all at home were when he left them and I was pleased to hear the news he told me as I had not had a letter from home then. He gave me some cigarettes and tobacco and then left as he had got a lot of work to do but he promised to come and see me the following day which he did. Well we saw each other nearly every day till I left to rejoin my Regt. Which I did on the 23rd January after staying two days in the convalescent camp. On the night of 22nd January we had a few drinks together it being our last night. I must here mention that during my sickness I received almost daily some of the good foodstuffs which had been sent out from England for the sick and wounded. On New Year's Day I had a small Plum Pudding and I liked it very much.

23rd January 1900

At 8am. I went to see my cousin's camp and bid him good-bye hoping we should meet again in the near future. At 8 30 I left De Aar by train en route for Modder River to join my Regt. And I arrived there about 7pm and reported myself to the Sgt. Major afterwards proceeding to my tent.

24th January 1900

I took over the duties of Orderly Sergt. for the week following, today being Sunday.

25th January 1900

Nothing worth mentioning.

26th January 1900

About 10am. I was placed under arrest by my Colour Sergeant for "Using insubordinate language"[25] to him and I quite expected I should be tried by Court Martial but luckily I didn't. At 11am. I was escorted before the Colonel to be tried and to my surprise I was dismissed with a "Reprimand" so I again resumed my duties of Orderly Sergt. At 12 noon all the Regiment paraded to receive the Queen's Gift of Chocolate and after everyone had received his present we uncovered our heads and gave 3 hearty ones for Her Majesty the Queen. The same evening the sum of £5-0-0 was offered to some of the men for the empty box and only a few were sold but not many for the greatest part of the Regt. Packed their box up to send to England. I was very pleased with my present and I mean to keep it as long as I live for nothing would induce me to part with it[26].

28th **January 1900**

Reinforcements began to arrive and continued to do so till the 4th February when by that time a column of about 30,000 troops had arrived to await the arrival of Lord Roberts and his Staff including Lord Kitchener.

7th **February 1900**

Lord Roberts and his Staff arrived quite early this morning by a special train and immediately proceeded to the Crown Hotel which had been prepared for him.

8th February 1900

The Commander-in-Chief announced his inspection of all the troops at Modder River.

10th February 1900

The 9th Brigade was inspected in the following order. North Lancashire Regt. 1st, 5th Northumberland Fusiliers 2nd, 2nd Northampton Regt. 3rd, and the K.O. Yorkshire L. Infantry last. We fell in on parade as he was inspecting the Fusiliers and on finishing with them he rode up to us and riding by his side was Lord Kitchener and behind them his body-guard. Our Colonel immediately called us to "Attention" and Lord Roberts addressed us thus:- "Officers, Non-Commissioned-Officers and men I am proud of you all and I have come to thank you for what you have done since you have been out here. I have read about your doings in the papers at home and General Pole-Carew who has seen a lot of service with me and who knows a good Regt. when he sees one has spoken highly of you and I feel assured that you will do as well in the future as you have done in the past when called upon. I must now bid you good-bye". Our Colonel then called upon us to give 3 cheers for General Roberts which we did heartily and the General touched his helmet in response as he rode on to the next Regt. And we dismissed to our tents. Immediately afterwards we again turned out to receive an issue of 1 quart of beer each at the cost of 1/-. I got mine and as I was writing my name in it I was tapped on the back and a familiar voice said "Do you want anybody to help you drink it?" and on turning round I faced my cousin who had just arrived from De Aar and immediately came over to see me. He came just right for a drink of "Oh my Dear"[27] and looked as though he could do with it for he was covered in dust from head to foot and I'll bet he had a thirst he wouldn't part with for quids if there was any beer knocking about

So after shaking hands I gave him the beer and he soon wrote his name in it in full and after a few minutes chat he had to go and as his camp was on the south side of the river I went a little of the way with him and then returned to camp.

11th February 1900

At 4 30am. We struck camp and moved to the south side of the river and pitched camp there. In the afternoon my cousin came over to see me and told me he expected leaving there very soon.

12th February 1900

My Coy. And "A" Coy. Went on detachment about a mile from camp and went on Outpost Duty for 3 days.

13ᵗʰ February 1900

Lord Roberts left Modder River with a column of about 40,000 troops and proceeded down country and nobody knew where he was going to for everything was to be kept secret. The Guards Brigade and the Highland Brigade went with him so the 1ˢᵗ Division was broken up as the 9ᵗʰ Brigade was left to garrison Modder River.

14ᵗʰ February 1900

The rear portion of Lord Roberts' column left this morning.

15ᵗʰ February 1900

I obtained leave to go and see if my cousin had gone with the column and I arrived at his camp just as they were preparing to take their horses to water at the river. He told me they were going after the column as soon as they returned from watering the horses so I bid him good-bye and returned to camp. About an hour later I saw the ammunition column moving off so I knew I had seen the last of him for some time.

16ᵗʰ February 1900

We returned to headquarters from detachment.

17th February 1900

On arriving at "Reveille" we saw the balloon was up and it seemed to be right over the Boer's position and we thought it very strange but shortly afterwards we received the news that the enemy had vacated the Magersfontein position and 4 companies of the K.O.Y.L.I. were immediately sent to occupy it. They captured 2 of the enemy in hiding with a lot of dynamite and other explosives to blow the railway line up with for they had been left behind for that purpose. The enemy who were commanded by General Cronje[28] must have left in a great hurry as all kinds of cooking utensils were found at their late position, also a few tents marked O.V.S.S. in large black letters which means Orange Free State. Plenty of all kinds of ammunition were also found as well as empty cases chiefly Martini-Henry[29]. About 4pm. we received the news that Lord Roberts engaged the enemy yesterday at Jacobsdal[30] and had driven them from that place with very few casualties on our side and General French[31] with a large force of cavalry had pushed on to the relief of Kimberley. About 8pm. we received the good news that General French rode into Kimberley this afternoon at the head of his force amid great rejoicings amongst the people at being relieved from their long siege. All day long we were the receivers of good news which we were all heartily glad to hear. The road to Kimberley is now clear of all the enemy and the line open for trains to proceed there.

18th February 1900

We left Modder River and marched northwards to Spyfontein[32] which is 13 miles from Modder River and 11 miles south of Kimberley.

19th February 1900

We were all expecting to march to Kimberley to-day and were in high spirits at the prospects of seeing the great diamond town of S. Africa but we were disappointed for we bivouacked at Spyfontein all day but we were hoping to go on the 20th.

20th February 1900

Another disappointment for us to-day for we bivouacked all day and at 5pm. we started on the march back to Modder River much to our chagrin. We halted for ½ an hour about half-way to have Tea and then resumed our march arriving at Modder River about 11 30pm. I was soon rolled up in my blanket asleep for I was pretty well tired. It is very fatiguing marching in the dark for we cannot see the ground clearly and it is very uneven out here. Now and again someone falls head over heels over an ant-hill and then in a hole. Many fellows fell down in a march with a sprained ankle and it is a wonder there isn't some broken legs as well.

21st February 1900

We crossed the river and pitched tents on the south side and settled down to camp life again. The 9th Brigade is broke up now.

27th February 1900

We have been doing plenty of work such as unloading and loading stores etc. every day since the 21st but nothing of any note has occurred. About 8pm. to-day we received the news of the surrender of General Cronje and his force about 4,000 strong to Lord Roberts at Paardeberg[33]. It was glorious news to us occurring as it did on the anniversary of Majuba Day for my Regt. was one of the Regts. which suffered severely on Majuba Hill 27th February 1881[34].

28th February 1900

About 12 noon we saw a party coming rapidly towards our camp from a north-easterly direction and as it drew near we could distinguish mounted men and a waggonette and news quickly spread that it was the redoubtable "Cronje" coming in under escort. The party stopped outside the "Crown Hotel" and we rushed to that place to have a look at the enemy's great general. A guard of honour was drawn up and he received the General Salute which he returned by touching his dirty old slouch hat. He was dressed in a seedy old suit of black civilians, dark complexion, long black beard and a cunning eye, looked to be about 60 years of age, short and very stout. Such was the great man who sat in the carriage which was drawn by 6 of our R.A. horses. A strong escort was on each side of the carriage. Seated in the carriage by Cronje was Mrs. Cronje and a small grandson, also Cronje's Secretary and one of our Generals. Mrs. Cronje was a little taller than her husband and looked to be a little older. She was of slim build and dark complexion, slightly wrinkled and looked as if she hadn't put water on her face for months. The whole of them on stepping from the carriage went into the hotel to dine and about 2 hours later they left for Cape Town in a special train under a strong escort. On taking their seats in the train it was noticed they looked decidedly better for the food they partaken of and a wash. On the train leaving the station they were hooted and jeered at by the natives but that was soon put to a stop to by the troops standing round for they let out right and left at the natives who were so misbehaving themselves.

1st March 1900

About 2pm the remnant of Cronje's force arrived here just as rain began to fall. There were about 4,000 of them strongly guarded by Guards and Highlanders. They were the most disreputable lot I ever set eyes on. Old bearded men, young men and even boys and women with children were amongst them, hungry, dirty and tired, dressed in all sorts of clothes which were torn and ragged. A few of the older men were riding horses which were ill-fed and could scarcely crawl along. All of them plainly showed what they had suffered and the majority of them were glad to be prisoners. They were told off to their tents which took a long time to do but was finally accomplished. They then all received a loaf of bread each and a tin of meat which they quickly put out of sight. We were installed guard over them. A sentry was placed between every 2 tents and sentries were placed at about 20 yards interval all around the outside of the wire which was placed all around the camp. The sentries received orders to shoot any who tried to escape. The prisoners were sent away in batches by train under escort on route for Cape Town and from there to Simon's Town[35].

2nd March 1900

Lord Roberts issued an order to the effect that any soldier caught looting or damaging private property would be hanged and the Regiment he belongs to sent to Cape Town to do Garrison Duty disgraced.

4th March 1900

A draft of about 200 strong composed of Militia Reserve Men and young soldiers arrived from England and joined us this morning. Rained very hard all day.

5th March 1900

It was still raining when we got up this morning but ceased about 11 30am. About 2 30pm a severe hailstorm came on and lasted about 2 hours. Some of the hail-stones were as large as eggs, such as I had never seen before.

13th March 1900

Nothing has occurred since the 5th. At 8am this morning "F" Coy left here by train to go to "Dronfield"[36] which is 8 miles north of Kimberley. At 4pm. the following Companies "C", "G" and "H" left here to go to "Dronfield" by road. We marched to "Magersfontein" and halted for the night.

14th March 1900

We resumed our march at 3 30am. And halted for

the day at "Merton Sidings"[37]. 4 30pm we set off again and marched to "Spysfontein" where we halted for the night.

15th March 1900

At 4 30am. We started again and halted about 10 30am. At "Wimbledon"[38] for the rest of the day. 5pm. we set off again and reached Kimberley about 8pm. and we occupied some spare tents which were standing.

16th March 1900

We did not march this morning but was allowed the day to ourselves but none of us was allowed to go into town so we could not have a look around the Gold Fields as so many of us was wanting to. At 6pm. we started on our last march expecting to reach "Dronfield" about 9pm. We marched through the town singing snatches of well known songs which amused the inhabitants for they cheered us heartily. Darkness came on as we left the town and shortly afterwards it commenced to rain and continued for hours. Our commanding officer, Major Fawcett lost the track no less than 3 times and each time we lay down on the wet veldt and patiently waited for him to find the right road. During all that time our waterproof sheets were fastened on to our belts and we were soaked to the skin for had nothing on but our thin khaki suits. The commanding officer was riding about with a long cloak on and some of the men kept shouting "After you with a loan of the cloak" and others were singing "How long will you be" till finally he gave the order for us to put on our waterproof sheets after we were wet through and they were no good to us. Well we eventually arrived at "Dronfield" at 1am. On the morning of the 17th, wet through, lay down to sleep on the wet ground and in the cold night air. That's what I call "Slow but sure death".

17th March 1900

Woke up about 7am. The sun was shining lovely but I was shivering with cold. We pitched tents and then I stood out in the sun to get my clothes dry.

19th March 1900

The following Companies "A", "B", "D" and "E" came up by train and joined us.

24th March 1900

A Company of Volunteers joined us from England so they became "I" Company. The 9th Brigade is forming together again now. We are doing 2 parades a day besides fatigues, outposts etc. Also we are to do 2 route marches a week.

29th March 1900

About 6am. We left here to march across country to Boshof[39] a small Dutch town in the "Orange Free State". We marched it in stages, marching about 4 hours in the early part of the mornings and again after sunset and so resting during the heat of the day. We arrived in "Boshof" as darkness was coming on the night of the 31st March so we had 3 days march. The distance we covered being 46 miles.

1st April 1900

We pitched tents and settled down for a short stay. We were busy all day putting stones around the tents and camp to make it look neat as we are camped just inside the town. The other Regiments are camped on the outskirts.

2nd April 1900

I went out and had a good look round the town and I must say it is a pretty place but the streets have been spoilt in places for the Boers dug trenches across them and stretched barbed wire across. The people are all Dutch, mostly women and children for the men are away fighting against us and the women and children are all in mourning for someone they have lost in the War. A lot of the houses are unoccupied but full of furniture etc. all topsy turvy. The town is surrounded by large kopjes and our outposts are to occupy them day and night to prevent any attempt on the part of the enemy to retake the town. I enjoyed my stroll around the town and found it interesting.

5th April 1900

The Bucks Yeomanry and the R. A. went on a reconnaissance in an easterly direction from the town, and about 12 miles out they engaged a party of the enemy and surrounded them and after a heavy fire had been poured into them they put up the white flag but immediately afterwards a Lieut. of the Bucks was killed by a treacherous scoundrel who was afterwards shot for his dastardly act. The enemy casualties were:- 10 killed, 15 wounded and 55 were prisoners. Not one of the enemy got away. They were commanded by General Villebois[40] who in reality was a Colonel in the French Army. He was killed during the fight. Our casualties were:- 2 Officers, 1 Sergeant, 1 Private killed. 4 Privates wounded. Total 4 killed and 4 wounded all belonged to the Bucks Yeomanry. The sergeant who was killed was Mr. Patrick Campbell the husband of the actress of that name who is so well known among the theatrical circle[41].

7ᵗʰ April 1900

We all left "Boshof" except the K.O.Y.L.I. who were left to guard the town. We marched to "Zwartkopjefontein" which is about 12 miles north of "Boshof". There was nothing to be seen there but we had plenty of sport chasing hares amongst the kopjes.

9ᵗʰ April 1900

The Yeomanry, R.A. and the Northamptons went out on a reconnaissance to the east. We took 3 days rations with us. We marched about 12 miles and bivouacked.

10ᵗʰ April 1900

We had a good march of about 15 miles and then bivouacked. In the afternoon it came on to rain and rained heavily all the remainder of the day.

11ᵗʰ April 1900

We started on the march back soaking wet for it had rained all night the previous night. During the march we got sniped at by some of the enemy on a kopje and one of our volunteers was slightly wounded in the right leg. We formed for an attack but we didn't have a fight for the enemy scooted on the R.A. sending a few shells at the kopje. We then continued our march for about 11 miles and bivouacked. At 4pm. we marched off again and marched about 7 miles then halted for the night.

12ᵗʰ April 1900

We marched to camp arriving there about 10am.

13ᵗʰ April 1900

Our tents arrived from "Boshof" about 8am. So we pitched them and settled down to the usual camp duties, outposts etc.

14ᵗʰ, 15ᵗʰ & 16ᵗʰ April 1900

Rained heavily each day but luckily we had tents.

17ᵗʰ April 1900

We received 4ozs. of bread each with our ration of biscuits. It wasn't much but it was very acceptable for it was the first taste of bread since we left "Dronfield" on the 29ᵗʰ last month.

18ᵗʰ April 1900

Went on outpost at 5 30pm. It is very cold at night now for winter has set in.

19th April 1900

Came off outpost at 6am. We had a bad night for it was misty and cold. I could not keep warm although wearing my great coat, and a blanket wrapped around me. As to getting a eyeful of sleep it was entirely out of the question. This afternoon some officers went out shooting game and they got sniped at for they went too far from camp. Luckily none were hit and they returned to camp quite safe. The sentences of 2 men who had been tried by Court Martial for "Insubordination" were read out today. The 1st was sentenced to 84 days Field Punishment No. 1[42] and the 2nd to 12 months H.L.

20th April 1900

About 10 30pm. last night we received the order to get up and put our accoutrements on and lay down to sleep with our rifles close at hand as an attack was expected at daybreak this morning for the enemy had been discovered in close vicinity to our camp. We were not attacked though for we slept till 6am. without being disturbed. At 11 30am we received the order to pack up our blankets etc. for moving. We struck camp at 1 30pm. and started off at 2pm. in the direction of "Boshof". After marching about 2 miles we suddenly heard the sound of the Boers' Pom-Pom and we knew we were being attacked. The General ordered the North

Lancashire Regt. to push on with the convoy to "Boshof" with all haste. Our R.A. commenced to return the enemies fire. The artillery duel lasted for about an hour and a few rifle shots were heard. We steadily advanced after the convoy and succeeded in arriving there safely about 8pm. It was a trying march for sniping was the order of the day. The convoy arrived there safely so the enemy didn't get what they wanted. For that was the object of the attack. They followed us to within about 5 miles of the town and then stopped and occupied some kopjes. We don't know the enemies losses but our losses were 6 killed, 17 wounded and 11 missing. We pitched tents and settled down to the usual camp duties.

22nd April 1900

Church Parade at 8 35am. fully armed.

23rd April 1900

We had a parade and done physical drill from 7 to 7 45am. Breakfast at 8am. Rifle inspection at 9am. Feet inspection at 10am. Parade from 4 to 5pm. for drill and then finished for the day.

24th April 1900

Same as yesterday with a fatigue in the afternoon.

25th April 1900

The usual daily routine. About daybreak the enemy tried to capture some of our cattle which was grazing on the veldt just outside the town and the alarm was given and the R.A. and Yeomanry galloped out of town. At the sight of them the enemy retired taking a few of the cattle with them but the remainder were drove into town by our troops. Later on in the day the enemy attacked the Gun Kopje but they scooted on the gun being opened on them. 1 wounded Boer was fetched in. A few of our scouts were wounded during the day and 1 is missing but he is thought to have been captured by the enemy. It seems like being in a besieged town now for the enemy are all around us and anyone who leaves the town gets sniped.

26th April 1900

The alarm went in the early part of the morning but nothing came of it.

28th April 1900

The Company that I belong to and "H" Coy. went on detachment to some kopjes to do outpost duty about 3 miles from camp.

30th April 1900

We went to a pond to bathe but just before reached there a mounted orderly came riding up and told the officer in charge of us we had got to return by Lord Methuen's order so we didn't get the bath after all.

1st May 1900

We returned to camp and immediately went and occupied some tents close to the Church.

2nd May 1900

I was on Examining Guard on the Kimberley Road at the entrance to the town. It was my duty to see that nobody entered or left the town without a pass and to examine all passes. At night a draft composed of 2nd Class Army Reserve Men and a few details from hospital joined us. Corporal Warren who was wounded at Gras Pan was amongst the details fully recovered from his wound.

3rd May 1900

The N.L. Regt. 5th Fusiliers with the R.A. and Yeomanry went out on a 3 days reconnaissance. In the afternoon I was surprised to meet a private of the K.O.Y.L.I. who was on furlough at the same time as me in October 1898. I was very pleased to meet him for he was present at a party at my home.

It is very curious that we hadn't met before for we had been in the same Brigade for 6 months and been through the same battles but hadn't met all the time.

4th May 1900

The following Coy's "B", "E", "G" and "I" went on escort duty with an empty convoy to "Frankfort Farm" which is 18 miles from "Boshof". We handed it on to some Coy's of the "South Wales Borderers" (Militia) who took it on to Kimberley. We bivouacked at "Frankfort Farm"[43] to await a loaded convoy from Kimberley.

5th May 1900

Bivouacked all day.

6th May 1900

The convoy we were waiting for arrived about 6pm. so we started on the return journey to "Boshof". It was dark when we started and what with the darkness and the dust it was worse than a London fog for we were marching close beside the wagons but could not see them. At one time we were marching between two wagons and I was at the head of my company when suddenly there was a rush behind and a lot of us rushed to the right of the road. The disturbance was caused by the bullocks behind us getting amongst some of the men and of course they rushed in all directions for it isn't much good trying to stop 16 bullocks. Luckily none of us were hurt. A convoy is 3 or 4 miles long, sometimes longer, composed of heavy lumbering wagons drawn by teams of bullocks, a team of 16 to each wagon and they travel very slow and are very awkward to manage. We marched about 12 miles and then halted for the remainder of the night.

7th May 1900

We resumed the march about 3am. and arrived in "Boshof" about 6 30am. just as it was getting daylight.

8th May 1900

The Colour Sergeant of my Coy. was admitted to hospital with fever and rheumatism. He was a very strict man and nearly everybody was glad to be rid of him for a time and he knew it too.

9th May

We have got the Provost Sergeant doing the duties of Co-Sergt. now and he is far better than the other one.

12th May 1900

I went on Observation Guard on Winserton[44] Road

which leads to the open veldt from the town. An old Crimean veteran lives close there and I had a good long chat to him. He was 75 years of age and a cripple. I was very sorry for him for the place he lives in was little better than a hovel. He belonged to the 11th Hussars when a young man and was wounded 3 times in the Crimean War. When he got his discharge from the army the Government granted him a pension of 2 pence a day and he refused to have it and told them he could do without it. He has been in South Africa over 30 years. He told me that different officers have been to chat with him and they are going to do something for him in the shape of a coffee stall to provide troops with coffee and other drinks. He was a gay old chap and I enjoyed my chat with him. When my tour of duty was up he gave me his address and asked me to write to him and let him know how I was getting on when we got further up country.

13th May 1900

We did not go to church for we were hard at work all day loading up a convoy ready for the march. The Munster Fusiliers, the South Wales Borderers (Militia) and the Scottish Rifles Militia with a battery of R.A. came into "Boshof" this morning.

14th May 1900

The following troops left here at 6am. on the march to a place called "Hoopstads"[45]; 2nd Northamptonshire Regt., "5th Northumberland Fusiliers", "1st Munster Fusiliers", "2nd Loyal North Lancashire Regt.", "3rd South Wales Borderers" (Militia), "3 Batteries of Royal Artillery", "1 Troop of Yeomanry" and a few "Kimberley Light Horse". Total strength about 10,000 under the command of Lord Methuen. We started off at 6am. and marched to Zwartkopjefontein and bivouacked till 3 30pm. When we started again and marched 6 miles northwards then halted for the night. We marched 18 miles for the 1st day.

15th May 1900

Up at 2am. and moved off an hour later. We marched 15 miles to a farm and then halted for the day. We had to do it in one march as there wasn't any water between our last halting place and the farm house. We did not march in the evening so we done 15 miles for the 2nd day.

16th May 1900

Moved off at 3am. and marched 12 miles then bivouacked. About 2 hours afterwards we received the order to obtain as much rest as possible as we were to move off again at 7pm. and do a force march of 20 miles before we got to any water. It wasn't very encouraging but like the old song "It was staring us the in the face" and we had got to do it "whether we liked it or not". At 7pm. we started the long march. It was then dark but "Tommy's Lantern" came up about an hour later. "Tommy's Lantern" by the way is the moon and we anxiously looked for it at nights when on the march. We halted every hour for 10 minutes rest up to 11pm. when we halted for 2 hours and had coffee and rum and a biscuit each. We resumed the march at 1am. and arrived at the farm house where the water was at 4 30am. A good number fell out during the march but we were all pretty nearly done up and no wonder for we had marched 32 miles in 25 hours which is no joke. After we had halted we soon had our blanket off the wagons and got down to sleep. I was soon asleep and didn't wake till 11am. when "Tommy's Extra Blanket" was shining lovely, I mean the sun but it is all the extra blanket Tommy gets these cold mornings and it is very acceptable when it comes up. During the day the Yeomanry brought 6 Boers prisoners into camp. The R.A. and Mounted Troops went on at 6pm. to Hoopstad which was only 7 miles. We remained in camp. I went on Outpost Duty but was allowed to sleep all night for reasons which I need not write here.

18th May 1900

We started at 6am. on the last 7 miles to Hoopstad and arrived there about 9 30am. The 6 prisoners rode on an empty bullock wagon and behind them rode 2 of the Yeomanry and on each side of the wagon 3 men walked so they hadn't much chance of getting away if they wanted to which I very much doubt was the case. On our arrival at Hoopstad we bivouacked and the rumour went about that we were to rest for 2 days and then off again. Passes were allowed up to 5 30pm. to go into town but some men who went into town to buy things stole more than they bought and of course passes were soon stopped and the town placed out of bounds to troops. I put a pass in but wasn't allowed to use it. What I can see of the town I think it is about the same as "Boshof" but covers more ground. The most conspicuous thing about it is the Church for the spire stands high above any other dwelling. On reaching here we arrested the Landrost[46] who hadn't time to get away and 2 Generals and 40 Boers surrendered to Lord Methuen. In the evening the following appeared in orders for all the troops to read, "From the Lieut. General Commanding at "Hoopstad" :- Please let the Column know that owing to its fine marching I have been able to arrest the Landrost here and have received the submission of Generals Preez[47] and Daniels and about 40 of the latter's Commando. Major-General Douglas[48] desires to express his appreciation of the excellent spirit shown by the men of the 9th Brigade during the long and very trying march on the night of the 16th and 17th May. The distance from "Boshof" to "Hoopstad" is 72 miles and we marched it in 99 hours which was a very good performance and would require some beating. At 5 30pm. I went on Outpost Duty again.

19th May 1900

I came off Outpost Duty at 6am.. It was very cold all night. At 7am. the Regt. turned out on parade and everybody's pockets were searched by an officer of each company and then each man's kit was also searched to find any of the stolen watches etc. which were stolen from places in town yesterday. Nothing was found in the Regt. though. Other Regiments went under a similar inspection during the day but I don't know whether any of the stolen stuff was found or not. During the afternoon I had a chat with two Latin Missionaries who spoke English very good and they told me that we were the first British Troops that had entered Hoopstad and they were surprised but pleased to see us. I asked them if any Boers had been here lately and they said that 500 of them left here on the 16th inst. and were going on to Pretoria to join the other Boer forces and that when the British reaches Pretoria they (the Boers) will drive them back into England. I must say that those 500 haven't been in contact with Tommy Atkins yet for if they had they wouldn't talk such rot. I wonder what they thought old "Bobs"[49] and his "Tommies" would be doing, sitting down and watching them do it perhaps. About 12 noon as I was waiting I heard a great shout coming from the direction of the N.L. Regt. camp and on emerging from underneath the bivouack I saw helmets and caps flying in the air and a mass of men shouting their utmost and a mounted orderly riding in the direction of our camp which told me that there was some good news. Instantly I thought, "Perhaps peace is proclaimed" but no. Still it was very good news we heard for as the orderly rode past he shouted "Mafeking is relieved" and immediately helmets and caps went flying in the air and we gave 3 good hearty cheers. Our officers were at lunch but the orderly rode up and handed the commanding officer a telegram and up flew all the officers' headgear. I cannot explain how glad we all were to hear that the brave little garrison was relieved at last and their long suffering ended. I know there will be great rejoicings in England when the news reaches there for everybody has been anxious about Mafeking for months past[50]. I trust now that the next time we throw our helmets and caps in the air will be on receiving the news that peace is proclaimed and that soon and I would like it to happen on the 24th inst. which is the Queen's Birthday.

20th May 1900

We left Hoopstad about 8am. and halted at 9am. doing 10 miles. The South Wales Borderers (Militia) was left behind because most of the stolen goods were found amongst the men. Some had watches, others shirts and were wearing them when searched and a lot of them are awaiting trial by Court Martial for "Theft". When Lord Roberts came out here he issued an order that any man caught looting or damaging private property would be hanged and the Regt. he belongs to would be sent to Cape Town to do Garrison Duty. I don't think these man will be hanged but they will be severely punished without a doubt at any rate. I don't envy them this bright prospect. About 6 miles from "Hoopstad" we passed a small farm house with a big white flag floating above it. We did not march in the evening. During the first week of our march we had 4 biscuits and 1lb. of "Bully Beef" per man for a day's rations but now we are only getting 3 biscuits each being on short rations. We had to be very sparing when getting 4 biscuits a day and now we are only getting 3 we are simply pining.

21st May 1900

We were up at 1 50am. and were off an hour later and we marched till 12 noon. So we must have done a good 20 miles and it was a very trying one besides being done on empty stomachs for the last food we had if I may call it such was about 6pm. last evening. Speaking for myself I was as weak as a kitten after doing about 15 miles and I felt ready to lie down and die for I was so weak for the want of food but I struggled on as the others were doing and managed to reach the halting place without falling out. A great many did fall out during the march completely done up. During the last 2 or 3 miles it was one continual cry from the officers "keep up in the ranks" and some of them spoke in bullying tones. They haven't got whips but they ought to have so that they could drive us along like mules or slaves. Some of them don't know when they have got enough out of Tommy for as long as poor Tommy can drag one leg before the other they will keep him going and he must not fall out until he drops. A private belonging to my Coy. was tried by a General Court Martial this afternoon for "Falling out of the ranks without permission". His sentence will probably be read out in a day or two. Such is Tommy's lot out here and our friends at home are misled by the newspapers simply because they don't know the true state of things but the truth will come out when the War is over and many a true story will be told by Tommy which will open the eyes of all at home and put England to shame. The following order was read out to us in the afternoon.

Special Army Order

A memorandum as under was issued from Army Headquarters. Rules to be observed by all troops serving in the Transvaal and Orange Free State.

> *I. All Boers when taken as Prisoners of War are to be sent to Cape Town for disposal. Any men whose cases have to be inquired into for political or other reasons should be sent through the Provost Marshall to the Military Governor of Bloemfontein[51] or to the nearest political officer.*
> *II. Boers who surrender voluntarily are to be permitted to return to their farms after they have taken the oath of neutrality and have given up their arms, ammunition and horses, receipts being given to them for any horses taken shewing their value. In the case of individual Boers who have been in command of the enemy's forces and have taken a prominent part against the British Government they are to be made Prisoners of War and their cases referred at once to Army Headquarters.*

III. *All horses, mules, donkeys, harness of all kinds, saddlery, carts and wagons may be requisitioned for the Public Service, but only such cattle, sheep and forage as are necessary for the supply of the troops and the feeding of the governmental animals should be taken, receipts being invariably given when owners are present on their farms and the property is voluntary surrendered.*

IV. *If the owners are not present, if they refuse to take the oath of neutrality, or if they are found to be concealing arms or ammunition on their farms, they should be rated as Prisoners of War under Pas. I and the whole of their property will be liable to requisition. A memorandum will be made by the requisitioning officer on the forms already issued specifying the approximate value of the property taken and this will be forwarded to Army Headquarters through the General Officer Commanding for future reference.*

V. *It is to be distinctly understood that no looting of any sort or kind, or unnecessary violence to the inhabitants will be permitted by any person is convicted of such crimes the Field Marshall will punish him with the utmost severity as Lord Roberts is determined not to permit such unsoldierly and disgraceful conduct.*

*By Order
H.E. Belfield Colonel[52]
Assistant Adjutant General*

22nd May 1900

We did not get up till 4 15am. this morning but we was on the move an hour later and marched 12 miles. We are doing one march a day now instead of two. The next town we shall arrive at is "Bothaville"[53] which is in the Transvaal and is about 18 miles from our present camp and we expect to arrive in their on the morning of the Queen's Birthday. We shall cross the "Vaal River" to-morrow and enter the Transvaal as the river is the border of the two Republics and we shall probably meet with opposition when we get on Transvaal soil.

23rd May 1900

We moved off at 3 40am. and when we had marched 8 miles the convoy wagons got stuck in the dry bed of a river and some of the troops had to pull their coats off and set to work to get them across and it took upwards of an hour as we have about 200 wagons. After all the wagons were across and the troops had crossed we halted and had breakfast and later on we had dinner. There was a kaffir's kraal close to where we halted and it was good sport

to see the Yeomanry catching fowls for they did
have a chase. Some natives chased a pig and it led
them a nice chase for about ½ hour and then one of
them knocked it down with a big stick and a fellow
of the L.N. Lancs Regt. went and stuck it with his
bayonet and it was quickly cut up. A drove of about
20 deer came rushing out of the thick wood close
by. They are known out here as "Black Bucks" and
they are a splendid animal, jet black. Some of the
Yeomanry mounted their horses and galloped after
them but they might as well have tried to catch a
cyclone. We could easily have fetched them down
with our rifles but we are not allowed to fire unless
at the enemy. At 1 40pm. we moved off again and
marched 7 miles which made a total of 15 for the
day. We done 2 marches to-day because of the
delay caused at the river bed. We expect to march
into a town named "Bothaville" to-morrow which is
only a few miles from where we now are. I have
forgotten to mention that just before we had dinner
we were suddenly ordered to "stand to arms" and
we thought we were in for a fight but nothing came
of it and we immediately dispersed again.

24th May 1900

Many Happy Returns of the Day to "Our Most
Gracious Majesty Queen Victoria". We moved off
this morning at 4 20 thinking it was only a few
miles to "Bothaville" but instead of being a few

miles it was a good 16 for we didn't arrive there until 11am. It was about 1pm. before we had breakfast. While dinner was being got ready for we was having fresh meat all the troops marched into the centre of the town and formed a square and we sang the "National Anthem" and gave 3 times 3 taking the time from Lord Methuen. At night we all received a tot of rum each and drank the Queen's health. "Bothaville" is 145 miles from "Boshof" and isn't much of a town for there is only about 30 houses there with one hotel which is called "Free State Hotel". We were not allowed in town to purchase anything on account of the troops behaviour at "Hoopstad".

25th May 1900

We were allowed to sleep until 7am. this morning and we thought we were staying there all day but at 2pm. we moved off and marched 7 miles then halted for the night.

26th May 1900

We moved off at 5 20 and marched 8 miles when we halted for breakfast and dinner. As we were forming up 3 Boers came and surrendered themselves and gave up their rifles which were "Lee-Metfords"[54] and must have been taken from some of our fellows for they are the rifles we are using. We resumed the march at 1pm. and marched another 8 miles making a total of 16 for the day. We are now marching due East and bearing towards "Kroonstad" so it looks as though we are going there instead of "Klerksdorp"[55] for that place is due North. I expect we shall join Lord Roberts Column and see some more fighting.

27th May 1900

We moved off this morning at 3 45 with the convoy which always moves off 2 hours before the column because the bullocks travel so slow. We halted at 9am. for breakfast and dinner having marched about 8 miles in 5 hours, almost a snail's pace. Soon after we had halted the column passed us. At 3 30 we moved off again with the convoy and marched to where the column was halted, a distance of 3 miles but it took us till 5 30 to do it. I commenced my duties of Orderly Sergeant this morning for the ensuing week.

28th May 1900

We moved off at 5 am. and marched into "Kroonstad" a distance of 11 miles. The town is situated in a valley and we bivouacked on the slope of the hill facing east. No passes were allowed into town. In the afternoon we had some bags of mail from the railway station for the railway runs through here to "Bloemsfontein".

29th May 1900

A day of rest for us. Passes were granted to about 6 men from each company to purchase goods but they all came back from town without anything for Lord Roberts Column had bought everything when they were here. They had left here on the 15th inst. The rumour is going about that General French rushed "Johannesburg"[56] with his cavalry and took the town. We got another weeks mail today and I got a parcel of cigarettes which had been on the way since February and which I had given up for lost. I was very glad to get them for I was in want of a smoke. During the afternoon the veldt all around the town caught fire and after darkness came on it was a grand sight and put me in mind of looking at the "Thames Embankment" from "Waterloo Bridge" at night but it was a great deal better. I expect the heat from the sun and the dry grass caused the latter to set on fire. It died out about 8pm. During the evening a fellow of the 1st North Lancs. Regt. played hymns on a cornet and all the troops joined in with the choruses, some 8,000 voices. The musician finished up by playing "Where is my wondering boy tonight?"[57] and some of the troops shouted "On the veldt starving for the want of food" and they were quite right for that is what we are wanting more of. It is bitter cold now at nights for we get up in a morning to find our blankets covered with a thick frost and the water in our bottles turned to ice and ourselves shivering enough to rattle the teeth out of our heads. Winter nights at home are nothing compared to these out here. It is rather too hot in the day but I would rather have that than the cold nights for I almost dread the night's approaching.

30th May 1900

We slept till 5 30am. and moved off from "Kroonstad" at 7am. and marched 9 miles when we halted for dinner, breakfast being out of the question altogether. I must here state that "Kroonstad" is 190 miles from "Boshof" and we completed the distance in 15 days. We were to move off again at 2pm. but was unable to do so as the veldt for miles across our front was on fire so we had to stay for the night.

31st May 1900

We marched off at 5 30am. and marched 9 miles then halted for breakfast and dinner. At 2pm. we moved off again and marched 11 miles which made 20 miles for the day. We received the news that we were having to push on because a Regt. of Irish Yeomanry were surrounded at a town named

"Lindley"[58] 24 miles distant by General De Wet[59] and 1, 400 Boers and they could only hold out till the 2nd inst. as they had already suffered heavily. We received a dram of rum each to encourage us I expect.

1st June 1900

We marched off at 5am. it being then quite dark as there is no moon. After doing 8 miles we halted for breakfast and dinner. Lord Methuen with 2,000 Yeomanry left us last night to push on to "Lindley" for having horses they could get along at a faster rate. We moved off again at 3pm. and marched 7 miles making a total of 15 for the day.

2nd June 1900

At 5am. we started on the remaining 9 miles to "Lindley" arriving there about 9am. to find everything quiet and no enemy in sight. We halted to bivouack on the left of the town and we could see a camp on a hill on the right of the town so I concluded they were our Yeomanry who had preceded us. Later on making enquiries I heard the sad news that the Irish Yeomanry under the command of Colonel Spragge[60] had surrendered to the Boers 2 days ago and the main party of the enemy left here the same evening with their prisoners leaving a few of their force behind to

protect their rear. Lord Methuen arrived here
yesterday morning with his Yeomanry and 1
Battery of R.A. with 2 Pom-Poms and engaged the
rear guard of the enemy for 5 hours. Their casualties
are not known. Some of our Yeomanry were
wounded. A large number of Boers and Irish
Yeomanry were found in hospital wounded having
been left by the enemy. The Irish Yeomanry who
numbered about 400 were on surrendering made to
change their clothes and put any old things on and
their horses were taken from them and they were
made to ride the worn out horses belonging to their
captors. We all deeply regret being unable to rescue
them but we should have so could they have held
out another 40 hours longer. We have now
completed 243 miles in 20 days and we are staying
here for a few days rest and a well earned rest too I
think. "Lindley" is a much larger town than
"Boshof" and is situated in a valley surrounded by
large hills the majority of them being natural strong
positions and a few men occupying them could keep
a large force at bay for hours for the for the ground
in front is all broken and difficult to get over as well
as a river of mud which must be crossed before
entering the town. The town is destitute of all
supplies except a little flour which we can buy at 6d
per lb. and we almost have to fight to get any of that
as there is a great rush for it amongst us to make a

few small cakes with. It is better than gold dust to us after living on biscuits 3 weeks.

3rd June 1900

The following appeared in Regtl. Orders late last night:-

Extract from Divisional Orders of this date –

The Lieut. General Commanding shares with his division the deep regret at having been unable to relieve the Regt. of Irish Yeomanry under the command of Colonel B.E. Spragge before it was captured by the enemy. Colonel Spragge stated that he could hold out till Saturday but had to surrender on Thursday at mid-day on account of the enemy having been largely reinforced by men and guns. The Division made a splendid effort. The Yeomanry and 4th Battery of R. Artillery with Pom-Poms having engaged the enemy for 5 hours at the end of the forced march and the Infantry having marched 44 miles in 51 hours. The arduous work fell on the 2nd. Batt. K.O.Y.L. Infantry Regt. in charge of the convoy. The Lieut. General thanks the Division for the work performed. The Major-General Commanding 9th Brigade congratulates the Brigade on their creditable performance to place on record his thorough appreciation of the cheerful manner in which all ranks responded to the call.

Reveille went at 7am. so we had a fairly good night's rest. At 8 45 the Division paraded for Divine Service which was the first since leaving "Boshof" and I did not attend that for at 9am. I went on Examining Guard with 6 Ptes. On the main road leading into the town. During the day I had a large number of passes to examine some of them being Dutch and I sent the holders into town under escort. I examined a natives pass and it said on it "Admit the 2 natives into the British lines without delay." And as there was only one native I asked him where the other was and he replied in broken English at the same time pointing to his left side "Dutchmen shoot, him dead on the veldt" so I concluded his mate had been killed so I hurried him into the town for I presumed he was a native runner with dispatches. At night we heard that Pretoria[61] had been taken by Lord Roberts's Force but thought it too good to be true. After dark a sentry challenged a man coming out of the town and in answer to his challenge "Halt, who comes there" he received the answer "Grand Rounds" but when the man reached us he turned out to be a man from the Regt. bringing us a dram of rum each which was far more welcome than the "Grand Rounds" would have been but the rum went down "Grand" all the same.

4th June 1900

About 6am. we were walking about in our Great Coats and a blanket wrapped around us to keep warm for it was and been through the night bitter cold when I suddenly spotted Lord Methuen coming towards us from the town. When he got up to us he said "Did you find it cold during the night" and I replied "Yes Sir very cold" and I think we looked it too. He rode on but about an hour afterwards he came back and we all sitting on the ground round a fire which we had managed to make out of a few dry sticks and dry cow dung but on seeing him we prepared to rise to "Attention" but he shouted "Sit down. I know it is very cold and I wish I could make it warmer for you" so I replied "Thank you Sir, but we have manufactured a bit of a fire", at which he laughed heartily and rode on into town. At 9am. we were relieved by a guard of the 5th Fusiliers and I marched to camp as I had nothing to do the remainder of the day and I wrote a few letters and posted them.

5th June 1900

Reveille was to sound at 6 30am. but at 5am. we were got up in a hurry with the unwelcome news that we were to pack wagons and march off at 6am.. Immediately all sorts of rumours began to float about and there was a pretty fair amount of grumbling for we were fully expecting to stay there a few days and we were sadly disappointed. At 6am. we moved off in a northerly direction from the town without the slightest idea of where we were bound for and we don't know yet for certain. We marched 10 miles and then halted for dinner. At 4pm. we moved off again and marched 6 miles making a total of 16 for the day. We heard that we are marching to "Heilbron"[62] to take supplies to the "Highland Brigade" under "Fighting Mac"[63] as their supplies are cut off and they are existing on one biscuit a day. "Heilbron" is 48 miles from "Lindley" and we are to do it in 3 days, 16 miles each day.

6th June 1900

We moved off at 5 40am. and marched 9 miles then halted for dinner. At 5pm. as we were preparing to move off again; bang, went a big gun and immediately after a shell dropped right amongst us and luckily for some of us it didn't burst. The Yeomanry were immediately sent out towards a sugar-loaf kopje where the enemy were supposed to have their gun. The R.A. got into action and commenced shelling the kopje and quickly silenced the enemy's gun but not before they had killed 1 horse, 1 mule and smashed a wagon up with their shells. The Infantry had nothing to do. About dark we moved off and marched 7 miles.

7th June 1900

We moved off at 6 20am. just before daylight but immediately it got daylight the enemy had another bang at us and our R.A. returned the fire with a Pom-Pom as well as Field Guns. The artillery duel for such it was lasted about a hour and our losses were 3 Officers and 1 Private of the Yeomanry. The enemy's losses not known. We marched 12 miles before halting for dinner. At 3 30pm. we started off again to do the remaining 4 miles into "Heilbron" where we arrived about dusk. Later on in the evening a telegram from Lord Roberts was read to us. It was dated "Pretoria June 5th /00" and contained the following news:-

The force under my command found the enemy at the 6 miles sprint yesterday morning after a 10 mile march and drove them back to a very strong position which they held obstinately until their right flank was turned late in the evening by General Hamilton's Column[64]. In a reply to a demand made in my behalf by Colonel De Lisle[65] that the town should be surrendered 2 Officers brought a message from General Louis Botha asking for a meeting to arrange terms. I replied I could only accept unconditional surrender and received a letter this morning tendering the submission of the town. My troops are now occupying it and the defences. A few of the British prisoners have been

removed but the majority are here or at Waterval[66].
Roberts

We all cheered heartily when the telegram had been read for it as good as said the war was practically at an end. Good "Old Bobs".

8th June 1900

We rested all day.

9th June 1900

At 3pm. we left "Heilbron" and as usual our destination unknown to us. The "Black Watch" from the "Highland Brigade" started with us. We marched about 6 miles and had a brush with the enemy on the way. Our Pom-Pom was again used. The enemy did not use a field gun so it is thought that it had got damaged. 4 of the enemy were found dead by some of the Yeomanry. Our only casualty was 1 Pte. killed of the "Black Watch".

10th June 1900

We moved off at 6 20am. and marched 8 miles and had a slight brush with the enemy on the way but it did not interrupt our marching. It seems to be a small party of the enemy bent on trying to make it uncomfortable for us by sniping etc. but they cannot do us much damage. We halted about 10am. for dinner with the enemy hanging about in rear of us but at a safe distance. We moved off again at 3pm. and marched 6 miles which made a total of 14 for the day.

11th June 1900

We marched off at 5 40am. and after we had done about 6 miles we became engaged with a force of the enemy about 4,000 strong who were in a splendid position along a range of kopjes and we thought we had got our work cut out to drive them off but our artillery let drive at them in grand style with Field Guns, Howitzers and Pom-Poms and kept it up for about 6 hours. The enemy replied Field Guns, using Shrapnel Shell. After about 6 hours artillery duel the Infantry and Yeomanry advanced to take their position by storm and to turn their flank but as soon as they saw our intentions they fled in a hurry leaving cooking utensils, clothing, food and various other things behind in their haste to get away. On gaining the top of the kopjes we found about 14 of the enemy awaiting us to take them prisoners as they had lost their horses. We also found 11 dead. The enemy must have suffered heavily for the kopjes were covered with blood but they took all their wounded away and as many of their killed as they could as they always do. Our casualties were about 20 wounded, the majority being Yeomanry. After it was all over we marched a short distance to a railway station named "Elandspruit" and here we found a few men of the "Derby Militia" in a hut wounded and they told of a battle which had taken place there on the 6th inst. which resulted in 40 of their comrades being killed, 130 wounded and about 300 took prisoners by the enemy[67]. It seems that about 4 Companies of the "Derby Militia" were guarding the railway at "Elandspruit" and on the morning of the 6th as the men were coming out of their tents they were shot down by the enemy who were on the kopje close by waiting for them. A train of trucks which were loaded with winter clothing for troops and other stores of all kinds were burnt by the enemy and a bridge and the lines were blown up. The damage done by the enemy was said to be about £10,000 pounds. The veldt was covered with burnt clothing, boots and stores of all kinds, also mail bags filled with letters, papers and parcels of all description were strewn about the veldt and the sight of all this brought curses and oaths from the lips of the men who saw it. We were not allowed to touch anything as we passed. The postman at the station was murdered and buried feet uppermost by the Boers. I saw his grave and his feet were just sticking out of the ground. I also saw the grave of the 40 men of the "Derby Militia" a stone was erected over it with the date of the battle on. We had some food and then we marched about 5 miles and stayed for the night. We received the order that we had got to get to "Kronstad"[68] for to-morrow night a distance of 25 miles so that meant force marching.

12th June 1900

We got up at 3am. and after packing wagons we got an issue of a dram of rum each and it went down grand and warmed us up a bit. At 3 45am. we moved off and marched 10 miles when we halted for breakfast. 2 hours afterwards we resumed the march and after marching about 9 miles we halted for we got the news that "Kronstad" had been relieved by a force who had arrived there by train from "Bloemfontein". We were all glad to hear the news and we were quite ready for halting. We were told we should probably stay here some days.

13th June

Reveille sounded at 7am. so we had a long sleep. About 9am. we proceeded to mark out the ground for bivouacking and then settled down to rest for the remainder of the day.

14th June 1900

Reveille at 7am. again. At 9am. we received orders to wash all our clothing as well as we could for we hadn't got any soap and it is doubtful if there is any among all the whole force. No clothing got washed though for 9 30am. we got the order to pack up and move at 10am. About 6 miles up the railway line we left 4 Companies of my Regt. to guard the line and unload supplies etc. from trains coming from "Kronstad" and then load them on convoy wagons to go further up the line as trains could not proceed any further on account of the lines being blown up. The remainder of the column marched about 5 miles further on to "Kopjes Station"⁶⁹ where we bivouacked.

15ᵗʰ June 1900

The Column is being broke up and sent to various places along the railway to guard it till it is repaired which will probably be a week or more. We are staying here unloading stores etc. from the convoys which are coming up. The 4 Companies which we left behind joined us about 10pm. We received a mail this morning of about 20 bags for we hadn't had any for a fortnight so we all got plenty of correspondence. It is rumoured we are getting our winter clothing here and that is good news if true for we are badly in want of warm clothing.

16ᵗʰ June 1900

At 12 noon I went on Guard at the "Kopjes Station" with 6 privates to guard the supplies which were being unloaded and which later on are to go by train to "Pretoria". The late Station Master's house is a large, nice building and it has 12 rooms in it but like all other buildings out here they are all on the ground floor for there isn't any upstairs rooms out in this country. We quickly made ourselves comfortable in one of the front rooms and had a roaring fire going for we were lucky in finding a bit of coal and it is the first coal fire I have seen since I have been out here so it is quite a treat for us. The room opposite to the one we are in has had wounded men in it for the floor is a ghastly sight all covered in clotted blood and bandages. The enemy had used it to put some of the poor wounded "Derby Militia" in when they were cut up almost by the enemy on the 6th. inst. The house is devoid of any furniture or anything else. The Station Master was taken prisoner by the "Shropshire L. Infantry Regt." as he had been giving information to the enemy so if he proved guilty he will be shot as he deserves. I must here state that we had been on the march just a month when we reached here the 14th inst. and during that time we have covered 325 miles.

17th June 1900

It was a very miserable night last night for the rain fairly poured down through the whole night. We dismounted Guard at 12 noon and as soon as I got in the Regt. I heard that it had been selected for convoy duty and we were to move off down the

Line at 2pm. and meet a convoy coming from "Kronstad" loaded with supplies. Precisely at 2pm. we marched off and we marched 18 miles before we met the convoy and it was then about 12pm. and we were all completely done up. It was 1am. before we had tea and we were ordered to move off again at 3am. but the Doctor told the Commanding Officer that if we did he would not be responsible for any of the men as it was too much for us to do without sleep so we were then told we should be allowed to sleep as long as we liked and we should start on the return journey at 3pm.

18th June 1900

We very soon got wet through but we soon got down to sleep after we had dinner. A dram of rum each was issued but I missed mine as I fell asleep before it was issued. And so didn't get it.

20th June 1900

We moved off again at 7am. and when we had gone 5 miles we halted and bivouacked much to our surprise at going so short a distance but on making enquiries I heard that Lord Methuen had got through to "Heilbron" with his convoy owing to being assisted by "Fighting Mac" and the "Highland Brigade" who came out of "Heilbron" and so got the rebels between the 2 forces who between them gave the enemy a good beating and caused them to beat a hasty retreat after losing 3 Guns and a large number killed and wounded. Our casualties being only 2 wounded. Naval Guns were used by our troops in the engagement. Owing to the assistance rendered by the "Highland Brigade" we were not required so rested for the day.

21st June 1900

Rested all day but at night went with my Company on Outpost Duty. I have heard we are staying here a few days but I expect we shall be off again in a hurry somewhere for there seems to be no rest for the 9th Brigade now. The War is over now with the exception of these few parties of rebels who are still hanging out but a division of cavalry is being formed to cope with them for we cannot get a good whack at them being on foot while they are all mounted but the cavalry will soon put an end to their little games. General De Wet is in command of them and once he is caught the game is up for he will be hanged and his fellows imprisoned and their property confiscated by the government for they are rebels and will get just punishment. It is rumoured that troops commence to go home next month from Cape Town and I hope it is true.

22nd June 1900

"I" and "G" Coy's went on escort duty about 4 miles and handed a convoy over to the 5th Fusiliers and then returned to camp. It was a nice march and I certainly enjoyed it and as we started early we were back in time for breakfast. The remainder of the day was spent by all in washing clothes etc.

23rd June 1900

"Reveille" at 7am. and after breakfast the usual rifle inspection took place and then we erected bivouacks and settled down to a day of idleness. Tomorrow being Sunday we are going to have Church Service at 8 45am. This is the best rest we have had since leaving "Boshof" 6 weeks ago tomorrow. I am certain my feet appreciate such a rest after being so ill-used for so many weeks.

24th June 1900

Sunday. Up at 5am. and on the march an hour later in the direction of "Heilbron" but we only marched for 5 miles and then halted for the day so it was only a Sunday morning's walk but before breakfast instead of after as civilians do. The Church Service was of course knocked on the head.

25th June 1900

Reveille at 7am. so with that we thought we were not marching to-day but at 9am. we started on the march to "Heilbron" about 5 miles distant. My Company was told off to do Right Flank Guard to the Main Column and the Captain detailed myself and 4 Ptes. To act as scouts and to keep about 1,000 yards from the Main Column. All went well for about 3 miles when suddenly about ½ dozen shots rang out and by the whistle of the bullets past us we knew they were intended for us and we were the object of some Boer snipers so we immediately took shelter in a miller which luckily was close at hand but knowing we should get left behind and probably captured if we stayed there I raised my head and looked around for the best way to get to some kopjes over which I saw my company disappear and which were some distance from us so I immediately decided to emerge from the miller one at a time and so form as small a mark as possible for the snipers who I knew would wait for us emerging from cover. Immediately the first man rose and ran for the kopje a shower of bullets followed him knocking the dirt up at his feet but he reached cover safely. Each one in turn ran for the kopje and each one was helped along by a shower of lead but I saw them all reach cover safely for I waited till last. When the last man reached there safe I rose and immediately I started to run I got helped along as the others had but I reached the kopje safely and found the men waiting for me. 2 of them had bullet holes through their clothes and I had one through my helmet and the bullet could only just have missed my knowledge box but a miss is as good as a mile and we were all lucky dogs. After a few minutes rest to regain breath we went on behind the kopjes and very soon came up with the company and we told them of the exciting few minutes we had had and they congratulated on our lucky escape. About ½ an hour afterwards we arrived in Heilbron to find the Highland Brigade still in camp there so they were having an easy time of it for they were there when we first entered the town, this being our 2nd visit there.

26th June 1900

Reveille went at 7am. and during the day we were employed on fatigues etc.

27th June 1900

Much about the same as yesterday unloading trains and loading up convoys etc.

28th June 1900

About 8am. this morn. some of the enemy ventured into the town as friendly and on leaving again they drove 65 oxen and 130 sheep before them which were grazing on the outskirts of the town and they got clean away before the natives who had been looking after the cattle gave the alarm. The usual fatigues during the day for us.

29ᵗʰ June 1900

At 2pm. we moved off on the trek again in the direction of Kroonstad and after marching 9 miles we halted for the night.

30ᵗʰ June 1900

Sunday. At 6am. we moved off and after marching 8 miles we halted for breakfast. After breakfast we went 6 miles and halted for the night and had dinner and tea. Later on we had a dram of rum each as it rained a little.

1ˢᵗ July 1900

We rested all day between some kopjes.

2ⁿᵈ July 1900

At 7 30am. we went on escort duty to a convoy of empty wagons to a place named "Katspruit" a point on the railway line about 20 miles distant. After marching about 5 miles we halted for breakfast and dinner. We resumed the march at 4pm. and reached our destination about 11pm.

3rd July 1900

Reveille at 7am. and we rested all day while the empty wagons were being loaded up. To-day is the 5th anniversary of my enlistment for I joined the Army 5 years ago to-day.

4th July 1900

At 5 30am. we started on the return journey to "Paade Kraal"[70] where we left the remainder of the 9th Brigade. And after marching 13 miles we halted for breakfast and dinner. We resumed the march at 2pm. and reached the Brigade about 8 30pm. with the convoy of full wagons.

5th July 1900

Reveille at 7am. breakfast at 8. Rifle instruction at 9am. and then bivouacks up. Nothing to do then until 1 40pm. when all the Brigade started on the march to a place named "Lesbenberg Stroom" distance about 7 miles. We arrived there about 5 30pm. and halted for the night.

6th July 1900

At 6am. we started on the march to "Waaihoek"[71] about 8 miles and arrived there about 11am. when we halted for the day. In the evening some troopers of the Yeomanry who were driving a herd of sheep close to our lines told our men that they could take as many as they wanted and it was not long before a large number of sheep were killed and dressed, dressed after a fashion for they were only beginners at the game and those sheep had a rough time of it. The outcome of it all was that 24 men were put back for trial by Court Martial charged with "Stealing Government Sheep".

7th July 1900

Reveille went at 7am. and we did not march during the day. The men charged with "Sheep Stealing" went before the General this morning but I haven't heard the outcome of it yet. The following appeared in Regimental Orders at night:-

"Discipline"

Extract from Brigade Orders of this date –

An unwarrantable act of stealing Government Sheep occurred yesterday in the 2nd Northampton Regt. The Lieut.-General Commanding ordered the weight of the sheep 450lbs. to be deducted from the *meat ration of the Batt. To-day and the offenders will be brought to trial by Court Martial to-day. Such conduct points to discipline being imperfectly maintained and the Major-General much regrets the disgraceful incident which not only brings discredit on a Regt. that has hitherto shown an example by absence of crime, but also reflects on the good reputation of the Brigade to which the Unit has the honour to belong. The occurrence is the more regrettable as the greatest attention has always been given to ensure the men are well fed and properly cared for (This order to be read to assembled units on parade).*

8th July 1900

Sunday.

Reveille went at 7am.. Church Service at 9am. and then a day of rest. The Brigade is staying here for a few days. The 5th Fusiliers went on Convoy Duty this morning to the railway line.

9th July 1900

Still in the same place doing fatigues, outpost etc. 5 boys of the N. Lancs. Regt. went on Convoy Duty this morning at 6am. towards the railway also. The following appeared in Regimental Orders at night:-

"Discipline".

111

Extract from Brigade Orders of this date (refers Batt. Order No. 3 of 7th inst.) is published for information:-

With reference to Brigade Order No. 3 of 7th July. The men of the 2nd Northamptonshire Regt. who seized a number of sheep without authority on the 6th inst. having honourably come forward and acknowledged their action and the C.O. being satisfied that the offenders committed the act through a misapprehension rather than with the intention of stealing Government property, the Major-General with the concurrence of the Lieut.- General Commanding direct that no further proceedings be directed against the men. The Major- General concurs in the view taken by the C.O. and has special pleasure in exonerating the men of the 2nd Northamptonshire Regt. of any intention to commit a theft of Government property owing to the high character which this Regt. has hitherto borne, and fully maintained since landing in South Africa. He cannot too strongly impress upon the Brigade the importance of avoiding anything approaching to looting a most serious offence on Active Service and which must bring discredit on the high reputation the Brigade has gained throughout this War.

(This order to be read to units assembled on parade.)

Dear Friends you see the Regt. almost became disgraced in a simple manner.

10th July 1900

Half the Northampton Regt. went on convoy duty 6 miles in the direction of Lindley and returned at night.

11th July 1900

The 5th Fusiliers returned with a loaded convoy from Kroonstad and they brought the winter clothing for the Brigade with them and we all got served out with a suit in the afternoon. The winter clothing is made of a kind of flannel and is very warm and suitable for the weather.

12th July 1900

We were to move at 7am. but the order was cancelled but about 4 30pm. we received the sudden order to pack wagons for marching. We marched to "Kwaggaspruit" a distance of 7 miles and halted for the night.

13th July 1900

At 4 30am. we started off and marched to "Doornkop"72 about 8 miles where we made the mid-day halt. We resumed the march at 4pm. and marched to "Battisfontein" about 7 miles.

, 14th July 1900

At 6am. we started off and reached "Kroonstad" about 10am. We received a 1lb of bread each to-day instead of biscuits and it was very acceptable for it was the first taste of bread since we left "Boshof" just 2 months to-day since.

15th July 1900

At 4 30am. we left and during the day we marched 15 miles along the railway northwards. It was about 8pm. when we halted for the night and immediately afterwards we received the order to parade again at 10 30am to march to "Horning Spruit Station" about 21/2 miles and entrain for "Krugersdorp" which is about 150 miles up country and lies about 25 miles north of "Johannesburg". At 10 30am. instead of parading we got the order to get to sleep and Reveille would sound at 1 15am. and march off at 2am. for "Horning Spruit Station" Reveille went as ordered and we marched off at 2am. arriving at the station about an hour later. It was about 11am. before the trains arrived and another hour before got started but we finally did get started on the journey. At about 7pm. we arrived at "Viljoen's Drift" the last station in the O.F. State and we detrained and had Tea. A mile and a half past the station is the great "Vaal River" which divides the two Republics and after crossing the bridge we entered a steep cutting and about half way up the incline the train stopped and then slowly went back to the bridge again, the load being too much for the engine to take up the incline. A waiting a few minutes another engine came and hooked on the back and between the two they hauled us up the incline and we had plain running again. I must tell you that we were packed in ordinary coal trucks as tight as sardines for there were 67 men in each truck and we barely had standing up room but we didn't grumble for anything was better than marching. Each man had his blanket and coat and we had got to get through the night the best way we could.

16th July 1900

We are now standing in "Johannesburg Park" Station and I must say it is the prettiest station I have ever seen. The town itself seems to be as large as London and the buildings are magnificent structures and almost a picture to look at. There are about 30 gold and coal mines in and about the town and a few of them were being worked. We had breakfast at the station. We all spent a very miserable night in the trucks for it was very cold. We stood singing snatches of well known songs for hours and till we got tired of it and then it became miserable for we could not get any sleep not being able to sit down even. After leaving "Johannesburg" we left the main line and got onto the branch line and after about an hour we arrived at "Krugersdorp" and right down glad we were of it for it was then about 11am. so we had been packed up 24 hours which was quite long enough. "Krugersdorp" is a fairly large town and a place of no little interest for it was Kruger's birthplace and it is here that a beautiful monument is erected in memory of the day the Republic gained its independence in 1881. This also is the place that Dr. Jameson and his troopers were brought to after being captured by the Boers and just outside the town is the spot where he fell into the trap laid for him. There are about 6 gold mines in and about the town but they are all standing idle as the male inhabitants are out amongst the hills raiding villages etc. and we have been sent up here to rid the country of them once and for all if possible. The troops in the town on our arrival were the "Gordon Highlanders", "Shropshire Light Infantry" and the "Welch Regt.". After detraining we marched on the outskirts of the town and bivouacked.

17th July 1900

Reveille went at 7am. and the majority of us had a day of washing shirts, socks etc.. We had bread again today.

18ᵗʰ July 1900

Reveille at 7am. and nothing particular to do. At 2pm. the following troops left the town on the march Boer hunting for the raiders were supposed to be 10 miles away. The "Shropshire L. Infantry", "Gordon Highlanders" and ½ the "5ᵗʰ Northumberland Fusiliers" with R.A. and some Yeomanry left the town in one direction forming one column. The "2ⁿᵈ Northamptonshire Regt.", North Lancashire Regt. and the remaining ½ "5ᵗʰ Fusiliers" with R.A. and some Yeomanry left in another direction forming the second column. Lord Methuen with the main body of Yeomanry went along the railway in a westerly direction. The second column under General Douglas marched about 6 miles then halted for the night. The march was over a hilly country but it was grand scenery. After we had halted the scouts came in and reported the enemy were in a position 2 miles away so we knew we were in for a fight the following morning if the enemy made a stand but the knowledge of that did not disturb our sleep one bit, most likely we slept all the sounder.

19ᵗʰ July 1900

Reveille at 5am. and after packing wagons we charged magazines and looked to the working of our rifles to make sure they were in good working order for a fight. We received the order, not to respect the White Flag if displayed by the enemy but to fire at it till ordered to stop. At 6am. we moved off and some of the fellows began making bets that the enemy would retire and we shouldn't have a fight. After going about 2 miles we heard rifle firing ahead and we knew that our scouts had got in contact with them but there was no fight as the enemy retired before we got up to them and we followed them up all through the day for they kept retiring before us but sniping was the order of the day. About 2pm. we halted for an hour to have a snack of food and then went on again. It was about 6pm. when we halted for the night at the foot of a mountain. Mountains by the way are very numerous about this part and we have a rough time of it marching. I believe if the enemy had the courage to take up a position on one of these mountains and make a stand we should not be able to shift them only by starving them out.

20th July 1900

We moved off this morning at 5am. and followed the enemy up again all day for they would not stand. Our artillery managed to send a few shells at them but sniping was the order of the day again. Our casualties were 4 Yeomanry killed and 1 Guide killed.

21st July 1900

Moved off at 4 30am. expecting to meet the enemy in a strong position and that they would make a stand. After we had marched about 10 miles we came across the enemy in a strong position on two mountains which commanded a pass and we knew we had got a tough job to shift them for it was impossible for Infantry to get at them to use the bayonet but the artillery gave them a terrible shaking up with Field Guns and Pom-Poms. Meanwhile we lay flat on the ground with the enemy's bullets whistling overhead. After about 5 hours the enemy gave sway and fled in all directions panic stricken which was caused by our Pom-Poms which were fired with great effect. When they fled we went through the pass but not before the heights had been scoured by our scouts. The enemy's casualties must have been great. Our casualties were very slight for the total was 12 killed and wounded. We camped for the night in a wood at the far end of the pass. The wood was thick with orange trees but they had been plucked and there was only a few stray ones on some of the trees but they were very nice and sweet.

It is 9 months today since we left England and still we are fighting. I must now end this book as it is full but I shall commence another as soon as I get one. I now bid my readers Good-Bye for the present.

I remain

Yours faithfully

Corporal G. Stokes

"God Save Our Queen"

Footnotes

George Stokes' Diary

1. This term was popularly used at the time by the British. The conflict may also be called the South African War, the Boer War, the Anglo-Boer War and the Second Anglo-Boer War. The Boers refer to it as the Second Freedom War.

2. The 2nd Battalion Northamptonshire Regiment had left Britain for South Africa in October 1899. On their arrival at Cape Town they became part of the 9th Brigade.

3. Cape Town is a coastal city almost at the southern tip of the African continent. It had been known to Europeans since the late 15th Century and its natural harbour used as a port by many trading nations.

4. Wellington is in the Western Cape Province some 45 miles from Cape Town. It is the location of an extant Block House built by the British to protect the rail line during the war.

5. De Aar is a town in the Northern Cape Province and was strategically important to the British being located at the junction of the railway lines from Cape Town and Port Elizabeth where they became the line to Kimberly and Mafeking.

6. The Orange River is the longest in South Africa. Today it forms part of the border with Namibia and Lesthoto.

7. Reginald Pole- Carew fought with distinction in the Second Afghan War (1878-80) and had been on the famous march from Kabul to Kandahar. He also served in Egypt (1882) and Burma (1886-7). Pole-Carew assumed command of the 9th Brigade after Brigadier-General Featherstonhaugh had been wounded at Belmont.

8. Lord Methuen had served in the Ashanti Expeditionary Force (1874), in Egypt (1882) and in Bechuanaland (1885).

9. Known as the Naval Brigade, sailors were heavily involved in the fighting on land in support of the Army. There is a memorial in Devonport Park, Plymouth which commemorates the men of HMS Doris who died in this war.

10. This may be a reference to Fincham's Farm, near to Wittiputts.

11. On the night of 23rd November British forces of around 9,000 men, lead by Lord Methuen, were marching to Kimberley for its relief. They were met at Belmont by some 2,000 Boers who attempted to prevent their progress.

12. Following the fighting at Belmont, the 9th Brigade again engaged with the Boers on 25th November at Gras Pan – also known as Enslin. Stokes' account of this fighting is very graphic.

13. 'Tommy Atkins' or 'Thomas Atkin' had long been used to denote the ordinary British soldier. The term was widely used in World War 1.

14. More accurately, the fighting actually took place, not at Modder River, but on the banks of the Rief River. However, as the battle

honours were given for Modder River the name has subsequently been used.

15. Lord Methuen made the point clear, describing the battle as 'one of the most trying fights in the annals of the British Army.' As one of Methuen's soldiers, Stokes takes the same view of these matters, describing the engagement as 'that long and terrible battle which was afterwards spoken of as one of the longest and fiercest ever fought in the annals of war.' Diary entry for 28th November 1899.

16. The Pom-Pom was so called pneumonically due to the sound made when firing. It could fire a one pound shell accurately over a distance of some 3,000 yards. The Pom-Pom was used by both the British and the Boers.

17. Magersfontein is located about 6 miles north east of the Modder River near to the border between Cape Colony and the Transvaal. On 14th December 1899 14,000 British troops fought with 10,000 Boers here.

18. Scholtz Nek, or Scholtznek, is an elevated ridge running between two kopjes or hills. The position was tactically important because of its proximity to the railway line.

19. Major-General Wauchope entered the Navy in 1859 transferring to the Army six years later. He served in the Ashanti War (1873), the Egyptian War (1882) and the Nile Expedition (1884-5). Wauchope commanded the 1st Brigade at Omdurman and Khartoum (1898).

20. The Rimington Scouts were one of several irregular units formed in South Africa during the war.

21. This is Stokes' own emphasis.

22. Kimberly was besieged from 14th October 1899 until 15th February 1900. Cecil Rhodes, who had made a vast fortune from mining in the area, was among those besieged in the town.

23. After Joseph Chamberlain, the British Colonial Secretary.

24. The uncovering of heads on such occasions was long established practice in the British Army.

25. Being arrested for 'insubordinate language' was a very serious matter for Stokes.

26. In 1899 Queen Victoria sent a gift of a tin of chocolates to all her troops serving in South Africa. Its inscription of 'South Africa 1900' was accompanied with the words 'I wish you a happy New Year' in the Queen's own handwriting. Not only was the tin not sold but Stokes then carried it throughout the remainder of his service in South Africa and brought it home to England where it remains in the possession of his family, still cherished.

27. The expression is old Cockney rhyming slang for 'beer'.

28. General Pieter Cronje commanded the Boer forces who had captured those involved in the Jameson Raid. He later fought in the First Boer War. In the Second Boer War Cronje was in command of the Western Transvaal region, including the sieges at Mafeking and Kimberly.

29. The Martini-Henry rifle was used by the British Army from 1871 until the end of World War 1.

30. Jacobsdal was a small town on the Rief River near to the border between the Orange Free State and Cape Colony. There was considerable fighting around Jacobsdal on

account of its proximity to Mafeking and Kimberly.

31. General John French served in the Nile Expedition ((1884-5) and also at Abu Klea in The Sudan (1885). He was widely involved in the fighting in South Africa, especially in the final guerrilla stage of the war. French went on to command the British Expeditionary Force in France (1914-5).

32. The area around Spyfontein was dominated by a range of kopjes or hills.

33. It was at Paardeburg that General Cronje surrendered to British forces and was taken into exile.

34. Their defeat at Majuba Hill on 27th February 1881 in the First Boer War had been a disaster for the British. It was the major and decisive battle of the war and a continuing source of ill-feeling for the British. 'Remember Majuba' was a widely used rallying call by their troops in the Second Boer War.

35. Together with Cape Town, Simon's Town was a major port through which the British brought men and supplies. Simon's Town was also used to site a Prisoner of War camp

for captured Boers before they were shipped overseas.

36. There had been much fighting at Dronfield as recently as 16th February 1900. It had been used as a base by the Boer forces involved in besieging nearby Kimberly.

37. Merton is a railway siding close to the scene of fighting at Magersfontein on 11th December 1899.

38. As a railway siding, Wimbledon could readily be kept supplied. It is about 25 miles from Spyfontein.

39. Boshof is a farming town some 35 miles from Kimberly. It is named after Jacobus Boshof who was the second President of the Orange Free State.

40. General George Villebois-Mareuil was a former colonel in the French army. He died bravely and this was recognised by the British from whom he received a full military burial, paid for by Lord Methuen.

41. Following the death of her husband, Mrs Patrick Campbell continued to use his name professionally in the theatre going on to dominate the London stage. It is said that

George Bernard Shaw wrote *Pygmalion* with Mrs Patrick Campbell in mind. She later went into film acting.

42. Field Punishment No. 1 involved the convicted soldier restrained and tied to a fixed object such as a gun wheel for up to two hours a day and for a period of up to three weeks. The public exposure was part of the punishment. Flogging had only come to an end in the British Army as late as 1881.

43. There had been fighting in the area in October 1899 during which the local Dutch Reformed Church had been burned down by the British.

44. Located close to battle sites of Spionkop in January 1900 and also of Vaal Krantz in the next month.

45. The local church building was used as a wartime hospital.

46. The term is used to refer to an official with local jurisdiction, a role rather akin to that of a magistate.

47. General Preez had acted as Adjutant to Martinus Steyn, the last President of an independent Orange Free State (1896-02).

48. Major-General Charles Douglas had served in the Second Afghan War (1878-80), the First Boer War (1880-1) and the Suakin Expedition (1884-5). He became the Chief of the Imperial General Staff for a short period at the beginning of World War 1.

49. 'Bobs' was the affectionate and widely used nickname for Lord Frederick Sleigh Roberts of Kandahar. One of the most successful British commanders in the Victorian Army, Roberts had served at the Indian Mutiny (1857), Abbysinnia (1868) and in the Second Afghan War (1878-80). He went on to lead the British forces in the Second Boer War (1899-02).

50. News of the Relief of Mafeking on 17th May 1900 caused huge excitement in Britain when it was received. There were widespread spontaneous public celebrations. Indeed, the word 'Maffiking' entered the language to describe such celebratory scenes.

51. Bloemsfontein had been the location of a conference which failed to halt the war. The city was taken following British military success at Paardeburg in March 1900. They later built a concentration camp nearby.

52. Colonel Herbert Belfield had fought in the Ashanti War (1895-6). In the Second Boer War he rose to become Assistant Adjutant to Lord Methuen.

53. Bothaville was the scene of ferocious fighting in November 1900 which lead to a rare defeat of the General Christian de Wet at the hands of British Mounted Infantry forces.

54. The Lee-Metford was used by the British Army in succession to the Martini-Henry rifle. This use was lasted only a short period before it was, itself, replaced by the Lee-Enfield rifle.

55. Klerksdorp was the site of a British concentration camp.

56. British troops entered Johannesburg on 31st May 1900.

57. The song *Where is my wand'ring boy tonight?* was written by Robert Lowry in 1877. It tells of a mother longing for her grown up child. It was popular with both British and the Boers.

58. It was at Lindley that on 27th May 1900 that the Boers had defeated the 13th Battalion of

the Imperial Yeomanry. This was much to the profound embarrassment of the British. The Battalion was considered a socially select unit comprising many from the upper echelons of Victorian society. Among the 400 men captured at Lindley were several members of the House of Lords giving rise to what became known as the Lindley Disaster.

59. General de Wet previously served in the First Boer War and had fought at Majuba.

60. Colonel B. E. Spragge had served in the Jowaki Campaign (1877), the Second Afghan War (1878-80) and the Burmese Expedition (1886-9).

61. Pretoria was, indeed, taken by the British lead by Lord Roberts on 5th June 1900. Now named Tshwane it is the administrative capital of the Republic of South Africa. During the war Winston Churchill was held as a prisoner in Pretoria before his escape to Mozambique.

62. During the third phase of the war when the Boers took to using guerrilla tactics the area around Heilbron became the scene of much action. The town was also the site of a British concentration camps.

63. Sir Hector MacDonald had risen from the ranks to become Major-General. He served in the First Boer War (1880-1) and fought at Majuba Hill where he was taken captive. In 1885 MacDonald was involved in the Nile Expedition. He also saw action at Omdurman (1898). MacDonald had a well-deserved reputation for his personal bravery.

64. Sir Ian Hamilton served in the Second Afghan War (1878-80) and also in the First Boer War (1880-1) in which he was captured at Majuba Hill. In the Second Boer War Hamilton saw a great deal of action and was frequently mentioned in dispatches.

65. Sir Henry De Lisle had fought in Egypt (1885-6). In the Second Boer he served with the 2nd Brigade Mounted Infantry.

66. It was at Waterval that British troops captured by the Boers were imprisoned and kept in extremely poor conditions.

67. Such losses may be seen as especially significant given that the men of the militia had all volunteered for active service overseas.

68. Kronstad was an important railway junction on the mainline from Johannesburg to Cape

Town and, as such, of great strategic importance in the war. It later became the site of a British concentration camp.

69. It was at Kopjes Station, in this same month, that the troop train carrying Winston Churchill on his journey back to Britain was ambushed coming under artillery fire.

70. Paade Kraal was the location for the Boer protest against British influence over them that lead to the outbreak of the First Boer War (1880-1).

71. The British located a concentration camp close to Waaihoek.

72. Doornkop became important as the place where Dr Jameson was captured in the ill-founded raid which takes his name (1896).

List of Photographs

1. George Stokes 1898

2. George Stokes and family 1914

3. George Stokes 1918

4. The Diary

5. A piece of khaki

6. Gravestone

George Stokes 1898

George Stokes and family 1914

George Stokes 1918

The Diary

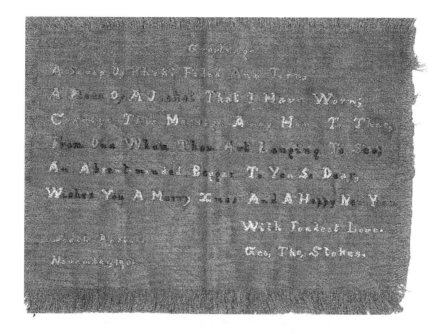

A piece of khaki

Gravestone

ABOUT THE AUTHOR

Stephen Huggins lives in East Sussex with his wife, Toni and their daughter, Ruth. He has long been interested in the history of British imperialism in late nineteenth century South Africa since first reading the African romances of Sir Henry Rider Haggard.

Proof

Made in the USA
Columbia, SC
28 July 2017